FROZEN IN TIME

What Ice Cores Can Teach Us About Climate Change

CARMELLA VAN VLEET

books for a better earth™

holiday house • new york

A ***Books for a Better Earth***™ Title

The Books for a Better Earth™ collection is designed to inspire young people to become active, knowledgeable participants in caring for the planet they live on. Focusing on solutions to climate change challenges and human environmental impacts, the collection looks at how scientists, activists, and young leaders are working to safeguard Earth's future.

For all the young people trying to save the world.

And for Marie, who changed mine.

Snowflakes are one of nature's most fragile things,
but just look what they can do when they stick together.
—Vesta M. Kelly

Introduction

IMAGINE you're a scientist. You're standing in a hallway of a research center. Next to you is a metal door with a small window. It's summertime and the weather outside is warm. But you put on a heavy winter coat and pull on a hat, gloves, and warm boots. You'll need them because you're about to walk into a freezer that's -30 degrees Fahrenheit. (That's thirty degrees colder than your refrigerator's freezer.)

Are you ready? Okay. You pull the handle on the door and go inside. Passing a small work area with table saws and other equipment, you go through a second door.

The air numbs your cheeks and freezes the hairs inside your nose. It's so cold that all you can think about is how cold it is! Then you look around the freezer. There are metal shelves from floor to

Scientist Paolo Gabrielli holds an ice core inside the Byrd Polar and Climate Research Center storage freezer.

ceiling. Everywhere you look, silver canisters are crammed onto the shelves, each four to five inches across and three feet long.

As the compressor that keeps the freezer cold hums, you pull one of the canisters off the shelf, open the lid, and carefully slide out what's inside.

It's a **cylinder** of ice. But wait. It's not just any ice.

You're holding an ice core. It's like a special type of time capsule! Usually, we think of time capsules as containers filled with objects and information about a certain era. People bury them in the ground so that other people can dig them up in the future. Ice cores are Earth's own frozen time capsules. They contain **data** about the **climate** in a particular part of the world over time. Only, instead of being created by people, they're created by nature.

This ice core is from Huascarán, a mountain in Peru. (Yep, there's ice in tropical areas!) The other containers on the shelves in front of you hold ice cores from other parts of the world, including Greenland, Tanzania, China, South America, and Antarctica. And each of them tells us something interesting and important about the climate in that part of the world. Some of the information in these ice cores is many thousands of years old. But no matter where they come from or how old they are, ice cores show us that Earth's climate is changing.

On the whole, Earth's temperatures are getting warmer. And these rising temperatures are contributing to changes like extreme weather, storms and forest fires, droughts that can harm crops, and other changes such as melting ice caps and rising sea levels. Some of these changes are part of Earth's natural climate cycles. But most of them are caused by humans burning fossil fuels like coal, oil, and gas. This long-term shift in regional and global climate patterns is what we call climate change.

Paleoclimatologists are scientists who study Earth's climate history. Like all scientists, they are problem solvers. And problem solvers always start with a question.

So maybe you're wondering, *What exactly is an ice core? And just how does ice tell us about ancient climates?* And maybe you're thinking, *Knowing what past climates were like is interesting and all, but what do icy time capsules have to do with the here and now, and the future? What can ice cores teach us about climate change?*

Great questions!

Keep reading. It's all pretty *cool.*

Natural Climate Cycles

From studying ice cores and other natural time capsules like **fossils**, and **sediment** cores from the bottom of lakes and oceans, we know that Earth has experienced climate cycles (or patterns) for millions of years. There are different kinds of cycles, and they often overlap.

First, there are cycles that last a long time. A Milankovitch cycle, also called a millennial-scale cycle, has long periods of cold and warm. The colder times are called glacier ages or ice ages, and the warmer ones are called interglacial periods. These cycles are influenced by changes in Earth's orbit. The changes happen very slowly, occurring over a period of anywhere from 10,000 to 100,000 years. Right now, the planet is in an interglacial period that began around 10,000 years ago.

Next, there are shorter cycles of warm and cold that last roughly between 200 and 1,500 years. These are called decade-to-century-scale cycles (or century-scale cycles), and they are usually experienced in a particular region as opposed to the whole planet. Scientists don't know for certain what causes them, but they hypothesize that things like changes in oceanic or atmospheric circulations are to blame.

And finally, there are even shorter climate cycles known as interannual and decadal-scale cycles. These may occur anywhere from a few years to a few decades apart. One example would be **El Niño**. This weather event typically happens every three to seven years and lasts from nine months to a year. El Niños can cause severe weather changes like higher temperatures, heavy precipitation and flooding, and even droughts.

COOL VOCABULARY
(in order of appearance)

cylinder: a geometric shape with two round (or oval) shapes at either end and parallel lines connecting the round ends. Cylinders can be hollow (like an empty soup can) or solid (like a candle).

data: facts, statistics, and observations collected in order to study or analyze something.

climate: the pattern of weather conditions in a certain place (or an entire planet) over a long period of time.

fossil: the remains or imprint of an ancient organism preserved in rock.

sediment: solid material (like rocks, dirt, remains of plants and animals, etc.) that is moved from one place and deposited in another by water, air, or ice.

El Niño: the unusual warming of surface waters in the Pacific Ocean that can cause severe weather changes.

PART I

FIRST, THERE'S SNOW . . .

AHH. Snow. The white and fluffy (and sometimes not so fluffy) precipitation that falls from the sky. While snow is pretty to look at and fun to play in, how it forms and where it falls are also important when investigating ice cores. So let's take a look at that process.

Two conditions are required for snowflakes to form: cold temperatures and moisture in the air.

When it's cold enough (32 degrees Fahrenheit/0 degrees Celsius or below), **molecules** of water vapor inside a cloud cling to tiny particles in the air, like dust or soot, and form ice crystals. As these crystals float around in the cloud, they run into **supercooled water** droplets. The supercooled water droplets

instantly freeze to the crystals, causing them to increase in size. Depending on the conditions, it can take the ice crystals from a few minutes to roughly half an hour to grow into what we call a snowflake. And when they get heavy enough, snowflakes fall to the ground, thanks to gravity.

 Because snowflakes form and fall under different conditions, it's true that no two are exactly the same.

In most places, snow that lands on the ground melts eventually. When the outside temperature rises and the ground heats up, the snow turns back into water and gets absorbed into the Earth. But if it snows somewhere that stays cold all the time—for example, in the mountains or at the North or South Pole—the snow doesn't melt, or it doesn't melt much. In these places, one layer of snow gets covered with the next layer of snow. And then *that* layer gets covered by new snow, and so on and so on. Over time, each layer of snow gets buried, and the layers press down on the layers beneath them.

Snow may not seem like it's heavy, but it is. *How* heavy depends on the type of snow. For instance, big fluffy snow contains less water and weighs less than smaller, wet snow. Wet snow occurs when snowflakes melt and clump together on their way down. That's the kind of snow that sticks and makes great snowballs. On average, a cubic foot of wet snow weighs between 10 and 15 pounds. (A cubic foot is 1 foot long, 1 foot tall, and 1 foot wide.) Several feet of snow covering miles of land would weigh . . . well, a lot!

See if you can solve

If a football field was covered with a foot of wet snow, how much would the snow weigh altogether?

Volume = length x width x height, so:

360 feet (length of field) x 160 feet (width of field) x 1 foot (height of snow) = 57,600 cubic feet (volume)

57,600 x 12 (average weight of a cubic foot of wet snow in pounds) = 691,200 pounds

691,200 divided by 11,500 (average weight of an adult male African elephant in pounds) = 60 elephants

So one foot of wet snow covering a football field weighs approximately the same as *sixty* adult male African elephants.

Now see if you can figure out how much one foot of wet snow covering your driveway weighs. The average two-car driveway is 16 feet by 40 feet. (Spoiler alert: it's not as much as an elephant, but it's still heavy!)

Maybe you can use this information to charge extra the next time you shovel a snowy driveway.

AND THEN THERE'S ICE . . .

Multiple layers of snowfall become compressed, meaning squeezed together, and grow dense. Density refers to how heavy something is compared to its size. Something that has a lot of **matter** packed together into a unit of space has a higher density than something that has less matter packed together in the same space. Think of it as a suitcase stuffed with clothes versus the same suitcase with only a few shirts inside. Or a milk jug filled with grains of sand versus a milk jug filled with marshmallows.

As the snow layers compress, the air pockets in them shrink. The snowflakes become round pellets. This granular snow is compressed into a grainy ice, called firn, that looks like wet sugar. This process is known as firnification. And then, after decades of constant pressure from the weight of layers above it, the firn

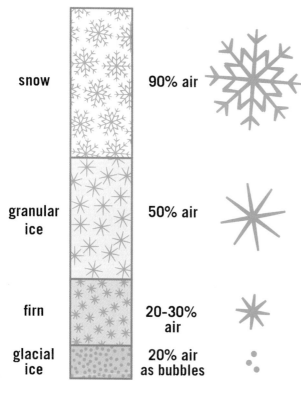

snow	90% air
granular ice	50% air
firn	20-30% air
glacial ice	20% air as bubbles

gets thick enough to fuse into a mass of ice. This ice is known as glacier ice, or glaciers. There are two main types of glaciers: ice sheets, which are also called continental glaciers, and alpine glaciers, which are also called mountain glaciers.

Ice sheets are permanent layers of ice that spread out and cover a large area of land. Today, ice sheets cover most of Greenland and Antarctica. But during the

An ice sheet covers most of Antarctica, including the Transantarctic Mountains.

last ice age, ice sheets covered nearly one-third of Earth's land, including much of the Northern Hemisphere. Today, Greenland's ice sheet is as much as 1.9 miles (3,100 meters) thick. That's roughly the same height as thirty-three Statues of Liberty stacked on top of one another. And on average, the ice sheet that covers Antarctica is 7,100 feet (2,200 meters) thick. But at its highest point, the ice sheet is 15,700 feet (4,800 meters) thick. That would be as high as fifty-two Statues of Liberty!

Alpine glaciers form on mountains and move downward through valleys. Glaciers are often called slow-moving rivers, and they can be found on every continent except Australia. It's too warm in Australia, even high up in the mountains.

Taku Glacier in Alaska.

But there are glacier valleys that remain from the last ice age.

Alpine glaciers are usually anywhere from a hundred feet to a few thousand feet thick. Some are even thicker. The thickest alpine glacier in the world, the Taku Glacier, is in Alaska. It's almost 4,900 feet (1,500 meters) thick. That's around the height of sixteen Statues of Liberty stacked on top of one another. However, due to climate change, alpine glaciers across the globe are melting at a faster rate than they have in the past.

Ice sheets and alpine glaciers may look like they're solid and still, but they *are* moving. While alpine glaciers move downward, ice sheets melt outward in all directions. Both move so slowly that scientists can't see the changes in real time. Instead, they "see" what's happening by taking photos or recording data over long periods of time. Ice sheets typically move up to twenty inches a year. And depending on the temperature, alpine glaciers move

How Do Glaciers Move?

Glaciers move in several different ways. One way is through **deformation**. As the constant and enormous weight of the ice presses down, the **melting point** of that ice decreases. This means the ice starts to melt at a lower temperature than it normally would if it weren't under pressure. (The higher the pressure is, the lower the melting point becomes.) And when the ice is near but just under this melting point, it can bend and stretch. It's similar to how steel and glass can be shaped when they are heated near their melting points. Deformation allows the ice to move around obstacles in its path.

Another way glacier ice moves is by sliding or slipping on a thin layer of water at the bottom of the ice. This water can come from meltwater that trickles down through large cracks, or crevasses, in the top layers of the ice. (The top layers are more brittle than deeper layers; plus, they are exposed to variable temperatures.) The water can also come from the friction between the ice and the ground, or from when Earth's surface heat melts the bottom of the ice mass.

about an inch a day. Some glaciers flow faster. Jakobshavn Glacier in Greenland is the fastest glacier known. It moves up to 150 feet in a day!

As glaciers move, they can change the landscape around them and create neat-looking formations. For example, glaciers are responsible for the formation of the Great Lakes in the American Midwest; the valleys, canyons, and jagged peaks in Yosemite National Park in California; and the Matterhorn in Switzerland.

AND SOME OF THAT ICE ENDS UP IN OHIO!

It might seem strange that there are ancient ice cores stored and studied in the middle of Ohio. But even though Columbus, Ohio, is far away from places like Greenland and Antarctica, it's home to a world-famous research program and has the largest collection of tropical ice cores in the world. Remember that lab we visited at the beginning of this book? That was the Byrd Polar and Climate Research Center!

The idea to set up a program at The Ohio State University dedicated to studying polar regions and the rest of the **cryosphere** was inspired by the 1957–1958 International Geophysical Year. The IGY was a project by almost seventy countries to expand and share scientific information about the planet. Following this effort, countries began working together to drill ice cores in Antarctica and Greenland, and The Ohio State University established the Institute of Polar Studies, led by Dr. Richard Goldthwait, a glacier geologist at the school. This program was renamed the Byrd Polar Research Center in 1987 after the university acquired a large collection of Rear Admiral Richard E. Byrd's papers. Byrd was an American polar explorer and the first person to reach the South Pole by airplane. The name was expanded to the Byrd Polar and Climate Research Center (or BPCRC) in 2014.

Throughout the years, the BPCRC has researched, drilled, studied, and protected ice sheets and mountain glaciers in a collaborative, or team, manner. Many scientists from different fields of study come together and work in the clean room, the cold labs, the machine shop, the cold storage facilities, and the Goldthwait Polar Library, not only to reconstruct past climates but also to predict the impact of climate change.

Two of the world's best-known ice core experts, Dr. Lonnie Thompson and Dr. Ellen Mosley-Thompson, teach at the BPCRC. Dr. Mosley-Thompson was the program's director from 2009 to 2018. One of the things that makes this husband-and-wife team unique is the fact that Lonnie primarily studies tropical ice cores, while Ellen mainly studies ice sheets, primarily in Antarctica and Greenland. Both are distinguished university professors and have been honored with numerous awards. Ellen even has valley depressions in Antarctica named after her: the Mosley-Thompson Cirques. Between the two of them, they know a world of information about our planet's ice.

You could say they have the world's ice covered from top to bottom!

Dr. Ellen Mosley-Thompson and Dr. Lonnie Thompson hold an ice core canister inside the Byrd Polar and Climate Research Center freezer.

WHY ICE IS IMPORTANT

It's said that the North and South Poles are like Earth's refrigerators because they help keep the planet cool. (The white snow and ice reflect the heat of the sun.) But climate change is causing Earth's ice sheets and glaciers to melt at a faster rate than ever before. So what's happening now that our planet's "refrigeration system" is having trouble? Here are just a few important ways that melting ice affects us.

COMMUNITIES

The water from melting ice sheets and glaciers flows into the oceans and causes sea levels to rise. Higher sea levels affect coastal communities by causing increased flooding and higher storm surges. (A storm surge is the above-normal rise in seawater during a storm.) These create dangerous living conditions for people and threaten their homes.

Places downhill from melting glaciers may also be affected by flooding.

CHANGING WEATHER PATTERNS

If the Earth's cooling systems start to defrost, the planet gets warmer. And these rising temperatures mean a change in Earth's weather patterns. These changes result in extreme winters and drier summers, which can mean more widespread wildfires that destroy hundreds of thousands of acres of land.

CHANGES TO THE PERMAFROST

Permafrost is ground (soil, rocks, and sand) held together with ice. In other words, it's ground that's frozen year-round. These areas are most common near the North and South Poles, and in areas high up in the mountains. One of the reasons permafrost is important is because it keeps plant material from decomposing. When plant material rots, it gives off carbon dioxide and methane, which are **greenhouse gases**. So if the permafrost melts and plant material begins to decompose, these gases are released into the atmosphere. Ancient bacteria and viruses might be released, too. Melting permafrost also means that any houses or roads built on top of it are in danger of collapsing.

Scientists studying the thawing permafrost on Herschel Island,
off the coast of Yukon, Canada, in 2013.

FOOD AND SHIPPING ISSUES

Changes in sea levels can cause crop fields to flood. Less food means more hungry people and higher food prices.

Melting ice can also open up new shipping routes. This sounds like a good thing, but more sea travel can mean more oil spills and more oil spills in places where it might be hard to get to and clean up.

WILDLIFE

Melting ice, especially at the poles, affects animals, too. Polar bears, arctic foxes, snowy owls, and walruses are just a few of the animals that depend on ice for survival. For example, polar bears use sea ice to travel over distances or to hunt, and walruses use ice to rest on while diving for food. If they lose their ice, then we lose them. And losing them, in turn, affects other animals (and humans) that depend on those species.

See if you can solve

Pressure is one thing that can lower ice's melting point. Salt is another. You can see this in action by placing two identical-sized ice cubes on separate plates. Sprinkle half a teaspoon of table salt onto one of the cubes. Wait a few minutes and then observe.

Salt is often used to melt ice on roads and driveways during winter. What else might be used? Brainstorm ideas, and then try the experiment again.

Some suggestions: sand, vinegar, rubbing alcohol, sugar, coffee grinds.

A field camp set up in the Dry Valleys in Antarctica.

The Dry Valleys

Ninety-eight percent of Antarctica is covered in ice. What about the 2 percent that's not?

The Dry Valleys, sometimes called the McMurdo Dry Valleys, are a row of valleys on the western coast of McMurdo Sound, Antarctica. Taking up approximately 1,900 square miles (4,900 square kilometers), the Dry Valleys are one of the coldest and driest places on Earth. The temperature can get as low as -90 degrees Fahrenheit (-67 degrees Celsius).

Any snow that falls is turned from a solid into a vapor by katabatic (downhill-flowing) winds that rip through the valleys, sometimes at 200 miles per hour. (The process of a solid skipping the liquid phase and transforming straight into a vapor is called sublimation.) The neighboring Transantarctic Mountains prevent ice sheets from entering the area, resulting in a terrain that's mostly dirt and rocks.

The Dry Valleys are the place on Earth that most resembles the surface of Mars. But even though the area looks barren and bleak, there's a lot of life there! In fact, it's home to a variety of extremophiles—or organisms that live in extreme environments—such as lichen and mosses, microbes, and microscopic worms called nematodes.

A cryometer is a thermometer used to measure very low temperatures.

SNOW, THEN ICE. WHAT COMES NEXT? ICE CORES!

Snow forms, then falls, and some of it eventually ends up as ice in the coldest parts of the world. But what exactly is an ice core? Simply put, an ice core is a sample of ice drilled from an alpine glacier or an ice sheet through a **borehole**.

Proxy Data

Scientists began keeping formal records of our climate around 1880, so they need to estimate certain things about the past. A proxy is a kind of stand-in measurement for data that we couldn't or didn't collect at the time. Ice cores provide a type of proxy data.

Paleoclimatologists use climate proxies, such as estimating previous temperatures based on observable changes in the ice. Other examples of climate proxies include **tree rings**, corals, and foraminifera (a type of single-celled organism found in both **fresh water** and salt water).

Fossilized pollen is another useful proxy for paleoclimatologists. Pollen is a dust-like microspore from trees and plants that floats around and gives some people seasonal allergies. Fossilized pollen is useful because some trees and plants only live in specific areas, like in high altitudes or in cold or warm temperatures. So if we find the pollen of a tree that grows in cold temperatures in the sediment layers in a warmer area, we can make **inferences** that the climate in that area used to be colder.

If you pressed a straw into a thick milkshake and then pulled it out, some of the milkshake would stay inside the straw. That bit of milkshake would be your sample. (And the hole left in the ice cream would be a borehole.) Of course, drilling for ice cores is more complicated than pushing a tube into thick ice—we'll learn more about the process in Part III. For the moment, let's go back to the laboratory freezer we visited before.

If you took one of the containers off a shelf, pulled out its ice core, and looked closely, you might see changes in the ice over

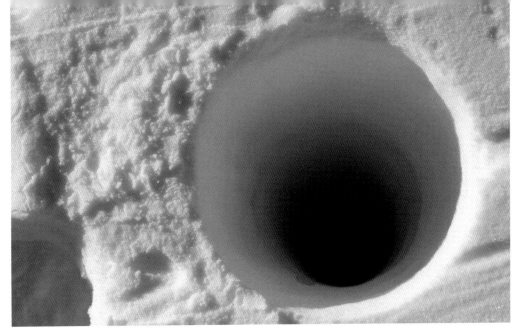

A close-up view of a borehole in the West Antarctic Ice Sheet.

time. Ice cores have numerous horizontal layers, or bands, that represent different seasons of snowfall. Each layer differs based on how much snow fell that year, the temperature at the time, and the chemical makeup of the atmosphere, which is affected by things like volcanoes and human activity.

This layered history isn't unique to ice cores. There are other things with layers that can give us clues about climate change. For example, the layers in **sedimentary** rocks, like sandstone and shale, and objects found inside rocks, including fossils and **glacier dropstones**, are useful to paleoclimatologists. There are **sediment** layers at the bottom of oceans and lakes, too. But the data in these layers is often limited to one kind of matter. Ice cores are different! Their layers contain *multiple* types of matter: water, atmospheric gases (inside the air bubbles), and sediment such as pollen, dust, and ash. This makes ice cores unique, and perfect for studying past climates.

Just as you might fill a time capsule with a variety of objects, ice cores contain more than a single piece of information. Keeping track of many types of data gives scientists a bigger and better picture of our climate history. They can't tell if something is out of the ordinary unless they know what average climate patterns look like.

One of the many changes scientists have observed by studying ice cores is the rise in carbon dioxide (CO_2) levels in our atmosphere. Eight hundred thousand years ago, the world had lower CO_2 levels and lower temperatures. These levels remained stable even after Homo sapiens appeared 300,000 years ago. But at the turn of the twentieth century, there was a big increase in CO_2 and temperatures began to rise. What happened? Well, humans began building factories, cars and airplanes were manufactured, and cities were growing. Human activity can and has drastically affected the climate.

HOW SCIENTISTS DATE ICE

Scientists study things like CO_2 levels inside ice cores, but how can they tell how old the ice is? How do they know, for example, that carbon levels changed when Homo sapiens appeared? Excellent questions, problem solvers! There are several techniques scientists use to date an ice core, or figure out how old it is. One way is to count the layers inside.

As we've just learned, ice sheets and glaciers are formed when the layers of snow from winters are compressed together. One layer presses on the next, and that layer presses on the layer below it, and so on, until the combined pressure causes the snow to turn into ice. Scientists can see these layers inside ice cores. Each layer, or band, represents a season. The band is wider or thinner depending on how much snow fell that season. Snow that falls in warmer months tends to be fluffier and less compact. It lets in the light more easily, so it appears as a lighter band in the ice core. Snow that falls in colder months is wetter and more compact. This results in a darker band inside the ice core. Sometimes these bands are easy to see without instruments. But the older the ice, the more compressed the layers are, and the harder to distinguish. For these, scientists use special tools.

Bands representing seasons inside an ice core taken from Greenland.

Scientists might count the number of a particular season, such as all the summers, to determine the number of years. But they typically count the pairs of layers—one summer and one winter—as one year. For example, an ice core was drilled from the top of a glacier, and scientists counted 120 total layers, or 60 pairs, in a 3-foot (1-meter) core. That ice would be sixty years old.

We'll learn about other ways scientists date ice in Part IV. First, we must make our way to the ice and find out how scientists drill for ice cores.

Don't forget to pack your gloves!

COOL VOCABULARY
(in order of appearance)

molecules: a group of atoms bonded together; the smallest unit of a chemical substance. (Atoms are the tiny building blocks of all matter.)

supercooled water: water that is below the freezing temperature but not in a solid state. It's often found in cumulus and stratus clouds.

matter: anything that takes up space and has weight. The three common states that matter can be in are solid, liquid, and gas.

deformation: changes in size or shape of an object due to applied forces or changes in temperature.

melting point: the temperature at which a substance changes from a solid to a liquid.

cryosphere: the places on Earth where water is in solid form (frozen). Solid forms include snow, glaciers, ice sheets, ice caps, sea ice, lake and river ice, icebergs, and permafrost.

greenhouse gas: any gas that contributes to trapping the sun's heat in Earth's atmosphere, known as the greenhouse effect.

borehole: a long, vertical column that runs through an ice sheet or glacier where an ice core is taken.

tree rings: the concentric rings in a cross-section of a tree trunk that represent a year's growth.

fresh water: water that's not from the sea. It has no salt in it and is vital for life on Earth.

inference: a conclusion based on evidence.

sedimentary: having to do with sediment.

glacier dropstones: pieces of rocks that were frozen to the bottoms of ancient icebergs and dropped as the ice melted, and then were buried in ocean or lake sediment.

SCIENCE IN ACTION: MAKE YOUR OWN ICE CORE

You can make your own version of an ice core at home.

WHAT YOU'LL NEED

An empty and clean Pringles can (You can also use a tennis ball container, or any narrow plastic bottle with the top cut off.)

Water

A measuring cup

Blue or green food coloring

Chilled seltzer or club soda

Gravel, sand, or coffee grounds

Cups to mix water and food coloring in

A spoon

A freezer

A cookie sheet or some other tray

Optional: fireplace ashes, plastic insects or plastic plants

WHAT TO DO

1) Pour ½ cup of water into the Pringles can. Place it upright in the freezer until the water is completely frozen. (Note: Do not put the lid on. Recycle it.) This will be your ice core's first layer.

2) After the core is frozen, pour ¼ cup of water into a cup, add a few drops of food coloring (either color), and mix. Pour the colored water into the Pringles can on top of the ice layer and put the can back in the freezer. You can choose how much water and food coloring to add, depending on how dark you'd like the layer to be.

3) Add a layer of carbonated water (about ½ cup). This will give you a layer with air bubbles that represents the air bubbles from the atmosphere that can get trapped in glacier ice.

4) Continue to create new layers by adding various amounts of water (anywhere from ¼ cup to ¾ cup), colored water, or carbonated water. In different layers, add small amounts (about a teaspoon) of gravel, sand, coffee grounds, ash, or insects to rep-

resent things like dust, volcanic eruptions, and other atmospheric activities. You can experiment with what you add. Each new layer represents a new snowfall. Allow each layer to freeze completely before adding the next layer. But make sure to leave an inch or two of room at the top of the can for the ice to expand.

5) When your ice core is fully frozen, carefully remove it from the can. You can run the outside of the can under hot water to loosen the ice or let the can stand for a few minutes on the counter so the ice can melt a little if necessary.

6) Lay your ice core on the cookie sheet and examine the different layers.

PART II

WHERE DO WE FIND ICE CORES?

Okay. Now we know what ice cores are and how they're formed, we've got our winter coats on, and we're ready to go. Where will we go to find ice cores? Hopefully you're up for some traveling!

Ice cores are found all over the world. (Except for Australia. Remember? It's too warm for glaciers.) Wherever there are mountain glaciers or ice sheets, scientists can drill for ice cores. Some places you might be able to guess, like Alaska and Canada. Others might surprise you—for example, countries in Africa and South America. The majority of ice cores that scientists use to study climate change come from Greenland and Antarctica.

Greenland is an island in the North Atlantic Ocean that is part of the Kingdom of Denmark. About 80 percent of the island is covered in ice. Its ice sheet is roughly the same size as the state of Alaska, and to put that in perspective, Alaska is more than twice the size of Texas.

It's cold in Greenland year-round. Two-thirds of the country lies within the **Arctic Circle**. In the summer, there is twenty-four-hour sunlight, and it rarely gets above 40 degrees Fahrenheit (4 degrees Celsius). In the winter, it's in almost complete darkness twenty-four hours a day, and the temperature can plunge to -30 degrees Fahrenheit (-34 degrees Celsius). Thanks to this chilly climate, there are dozens of sites in Greenland where scientists drill for ice cores. About one-third of the world's studied ice cores are retrieved from Greenland.

Earth with the Arctic region, including Greenland and sea ice, shown near the top. (Created 2007.)

The only ice sheet bigger than Greenland's is the one covering Antarctica. Around 5.5 million square miles, Antarctica is about one and a half times bigger than the United States. It's almost entirely inside the Antarctic Circle and almost entirely covered in thick ice. Like Greenland, Antarctica experiences seasons of twenty-four-hour darkness or light, and it is cold year-round. The average temperature ranges from 14 degrees Fahrenheit (-10 degrees Celsius) to -75 degrees Fahrenheit (-60 degrees Celsius) at its higher **elevations**.

Earth with Antarctica and sea ice shown near the bottom. (Created 2007.)

These temperatures make Antarctica the coldest place on Earth. This frozen continent holds other records, too: windiest, iciest, and driest.

Antarctica is considered the world's largest desert.

And because it is far away from other continents' air pollution and has strict environmental laws, Antarctica is widely considered the cleanest place on Earth.

No indigenous people live in Antarctica, but anywhere from 1,000 to 5,000 scientists take up temporary residence at various research stations throughout the year. These stations are like small towns—they have landing strips for planes, and buildings such as laboratories, firehouses, power plants, stores, doctors' offices, chapels, warehouses, and dormitories. For many years, there were even small schools for researchers' children at two of the stations!

Greenland

At 836,300 square miles, Greenland is the world's largest island that's not a continent. But it is also one of the least densely populated countries, with only 55,000 people. Most of the population is of Inuit descent, meaning they are a member of an indigenous (native) group, living in small towns along the coastline.

While almost all of Greenland is covered in ice, the rest of the country is a tundra. A tundra is a large, cold, windy, snowy, and treeless area. The ice and tundra make traveling difficult, so none of Greenland's towns are connected by roads. Can you figure out how people get from town to another? Yep! By boat.

Another interesting thing about Greenland is what's under the ice. Besides land features like mountains and canyons, there are remnants of visitors from space. No, not that kind of visitor. In 2018, glaciologists discovered a large crater that was likely formed when an asteroid hit Earth, long before the ice formed.

Antarctica is valuable when it comes to ice cores because it has *7 million cubic miles* of ice. Some of it is two million years old—or maybe even older. Antarctica also has about 90 percent of the world's **fresh water**.

Ice cores taken from Antarctica, Greenland, and other arctic places are called polar ice cores.

See if you can solve

Using the information below, how many days would it take you to walk Greenland's Arctic Circle Trail?

The trail is approximately 100 miles long.

Assume you can hike 5 miles in a day. (This may not seem like a lot, but remember, the terrain is fairly difficult and you'd be carrying a backpack with your supplies.)

So 100 miles divided by 5 miles per day = 20 days.

That's almost three weeks!

Now figure out how many days it would take if you could hike faster because either 1) you're super strong, or 2) you were able to sweet-talk someone into carrying your backpack.

Spoiler alert: it'll still probably take longer than a week.

The Arctic and Antarctic Circles

Have you ever seen a globe or a photo of Earth from space? Our planet is a sphere (a solid round object), and it orbits around the sun on a tilted **axis**. Around the middle of Earth is an imaginary line called the equator. The equator divides the planet into two halves, or hemispheres: the Northern Hemisphere and the Southern Hemisphere. Starting from the equator and moving out in both directions (running horizontally) are more imaginary **parallel** lines called latitudes. There is an imaginary line that goes from the top of the sphere to the bottom, too. It's called the prime meridian. There are also imaginary lines called longitudes, which move around the globe in both directions (running vertically).

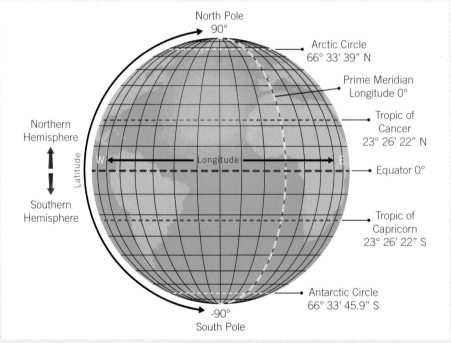

Latitude and longitude lines run lengthwise and widthwise across the Earth's spherical surface, making circles. We use the intersections of these lines to pinpoint locations all over the world with a notation system called DMS.

DMS

You might have learned that circles have 360 degrees. The equator is the 0-degree mark of latitude, and the prime meridian is the 0-degree mark of longitude. Each of those degrees is further split into 60 minutes, and each of those minutes is split into 60 seconds. (Imagine the face of a clock.) For example, the coordinates for Central Park in New York City are 40° 47' 6.3276" N and 73° 58' 5.8260" W. This means Central Park is roughly 40 degrees, 47 minutes, and 6 seconds north of the equator, and 73 degrees, 58 minutes, and 5 seconds west of the prime meridian.

The Arctic Circle is the latitude line that goes around Earth at approximately 66° 30' N, creating an imaginary circle at the top of Earth's sphere. And the Antarctic Circle is the latitude line that goes around Earth at approximately 66° 30' S, creating an imaginary circle at the bottom of the planet's sphere. In the centers of these imaginary circles are the North and South Poles, respectively.

GUESS WHAT. THERE ARE ICE CORES IN THE TROPICS, TOO!

We usually think of ice in cold places. But some places with warm weather also have ice high up in the mountains.

Remember the equator, the invisible line that goes around the middle of Earth? At 23.5 degrees north of the equator is the latitude known as the Tropic of Cancer. At 23.5 degrees south of the equator is the latitude known as the Tropic of Capricorn. Between these two latitudes is a region called the tropics. It is roughly the middle band of our planet. The tropics are typically warm and rainy all year round. Scientists call ice cores taken from these areas tropical ice cores.

Although scientists began drilling and studying ice cores in the 1960s, no one studied ice outside the polar regions for another decade. That's when a small group of scientists, including Dr. Lonnie Thompson, started asking questions like: How do tropical weather events affect alpine glacier ice?

Problem solvers always start with a question!

Dr. Thompson and his colleagues began taking trips to the Quelccaya Ice Cap in the Andes mountains in Peru, where they did some preliminary research and searched for areas to drill. There were a lot of unknowns. For example: How hard would it be to get to the top of the mountain? Would the equipment work at that elevation? How would they get the ice back down? In 1983, Dr. Thompson and his team successfully drilled the first tropical ice core. (They actually drilled two cores!) He and his team weren't able to bring back the Quelccaya ice cores frozen, though. At the time, there wasn't the technology to do so. Instead, they cut the ice with handsaws, melted it, and stored the water in 6,000 sealed bottles. This water provided information about climate all the way back to 1500 AD, and included ash from the 1600 eruption of the Huaynaputina volcano in southern Peru.

Since then, scientists have drilled ice cores in other parts of Peru and in tropical regions including Kilimanjaro (Tanzania) and Papua (Indonesia).

THE THIRD POLE

We've all heard of the North and South Poles. But there's also

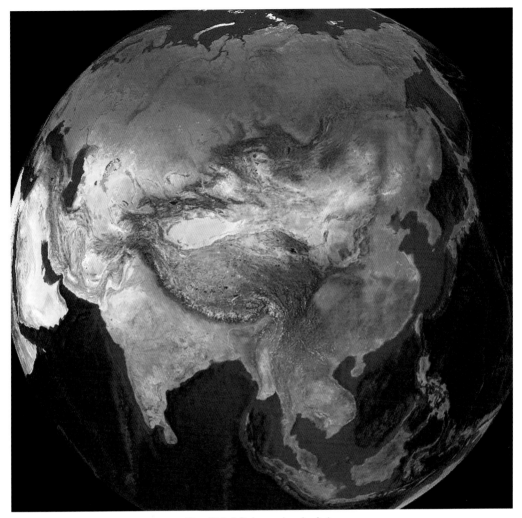

The Third Pole region in Asia.

a region called the Third Pole. The Third Pole is home to the Tibetan **Plateau** and to the Himalayan, Pamir-Hindu Kush, and Tien Shan mountain ranges. Clocking in at approximately 1,930,510 square miles (5 million square kilometers), this area is almost three times larger than Alaska. It is the largest and highest mountainous region in the world, with an average elevation around 13,120 feet (4,000 meters). The Third Pole gets its nickname from the fact that it holds the world's third-largest amount of ice, second to the North and South Poles. Ice cores from this area are called low-latitude or mid-latitude ice cores.

The cryosphere in the tropics and places like the Third Pole is sensitive. Even a small temperature change can cause glaciers to retreat. When scientists say a glacier is retreating, they mean there's not enough precipitation, or snow, to replace the ice that's melting off the glacier. (Retreating doesn't mean a glacier is moving uphill. Glaciers are always moving downhill, even though it may not look like it.)

Unfortunately, most of the world's glaciers are melting faster than they used to. In 2021, scientists conducted a study using 3D satellite photos and confirmed that Earth is losing massive amounts of ice. Between 2000 and 2019, we lost an average of 267 **gigatons** of glacier ice *each year.* And a 2019 report from the IPCC (Intergovernmental Panel on Climate Change) predicts that two-thirds of the ice in the Third Pole region will be gone in less than a hundred years. Even if we immediately start making drastic changes to improve how we take care of our planet, we are still going to lose one-third of that ice.

Pollution is a big part of this terrifying trend. Soot, dust, and other particles settle on top of the snow that sits on top of the ice, and this "darker" snow absorbs heat from the sun, causing the ice to melt faster. Have you ever worn a black sweater on a warm day? You probably got hot and sweaty quickly. That's because, while lighter-colored materials reflect heat, darker-colored materials absorb it. The same is true for things in nature. Plus, meltwater can damage the lower layers of ice. And when this happens, the data the ice might contain is damaged, too.

Maybe you're asking, *If Greenland and Antarctica have a*

Glaciers all over the world, including those in the Third Pole, are retreating. This photo showing the Qori Kalis Glacier in Peru is from 1978. (Peru is located in South America.)

A photo of the Qori Kalis Glacier from 2018. In just 40 years, the glacier retreated nearly three-quarters of a mile.

ton of ice, why do scientists care about tropical ice cores or ice from the Third Pole? The answer is that these ice cores can tell us things that polar ice cores can't. Tropical ice cores give us information on El Niño and **monsoons**, dangerous weather events that occur in tropical areas. And just as importantly, they tell us about the climate patterns of places where a large number

Scientists drilling a glacier 22,000 feet above sea level on the Tibetan Plateau.

of people live. Remember, Greenland has around 55,000 people and Antarctica has no indigenous people. Around *40 percent* of the world's population live in the tropics and near the Third Pole. That 40 percent represents more than 3.5 billion people! The way climate is changing in these areas is vital to understanding global climate changes and their impact.

Melting glaciers can disrupt a region in many ways, including dangerous flooding. Normally, meltwater sits in large basins (bowl-shaped dips or depressions in land surfaces) up in the mountains. When these glacier lakes overflow, they flood communities downhill. Flooding destroys crops meant for humans, but also for livestock, such as yaks. Yaks are a food source in **Tibet**, and they're used to transport goods and medicine.

Floodwater also disrupts the habitats of local plants and wildlife. The Third Pole is home to the largest number of **endemic species** in any region of the world, as well as endangered animals like the red panda and the snow leopard. If the glaciers in the area are in danger, so are these plants and animals.

Because the ice cores in the Third Pole and other tropical and low-latitude glaciers and the data that their ice cores provide are so important, scientists are racing to retrieve them before they're gone. For example, in 2000, Dr. Lonnie Thompson and his team drilled an ice core in the Fürtwangler Glacier on Mount Kilimanjaro. They left a pole in the hole to mark the ice's depth: 31 feet. Thirteen years later, a scientist named Doug Hardy measured the ice when he visited the site. The glacier had lost twenty feet of ice!

Environmental Migrants

Climate change affects just about everything on the planet. It even affects where people live. As countries face droughts, floods, rising temperatures, and rising sea levels, parts of the world are quickly becoming uninhabitable. This is especially true in places in the Third Pole, where even small changes in climate can have big effects and the governments don't have the resources to deal with the needs of large populations. Environmental migrants are people who are displaced because of climate change. Millions of people have already been forced from their homes due to wildfires, hurricanes, cyclones, and pollution, and many experts predict that 200 million people will become environmental migrants by the 2050s. (Some experts estimate that the number could be as high as one *billion*!)

Environmental migration will be a growing challenge in the future, affecting both wealthy and poor countries. Governments around the world will need to work together, share resources, and be proactive.

See if you can solve

Between 2000 and 2019, Earth lost an average of 267 gigatons of glacier ice each year. A gigaton is one billion metric tons. How many Olympic-sized pools would it take to hold one gigaton of ice?

Clue: One Olympic-sized pool holds 2,500 metric tons of water.

It would take 400,000 Olympic-sized pools to hold one gigaton of ice. $1,000,000,000 \div 2,500 = 400,000$

Sea Ice

Sea ice is just what it sounds like: ice that forms in the ocean from frozen seawater. There is sea ice in the Arctic Ocean at the North Pole, as well as in the Antarctic Ocean, or Southern Ocean. Don't confuse sea ice with icebergs, which also float in the oceans! Icebergs are chunks of glaciers (fresh water) that have broken off into the sea.

Scientists drill ice cores from sea ice to study how climate change is affecting the oceans. For instance, they track algae and **zooplankton**. If these microorganisms are detected outside their native area, scientists can tell how far the sea ice is flowing. This is important information, since many animals, like krill, fish, seals, and whales, rely on algae and zooplankton for food.

GETTING READY

Collecting ice cores is extreme business. It's frigid and windy and often dangerous to get to and to work on ice sheets and glaciers. Regardless of where scientists go, collecting ice cores takes a lot of time, a lot of money, a lot of people, and a lot of preparation!

Scientists take many things into consideration when planning their next **expedition**. First and foremost, they choose a location based on the data they're looking for. They might want to know:

- Are greenhouse gas or carbon levels changing in a particular area?
- How have humans impacted the cryosphere in more populated areas?

- How is human activity currently affecting ice sheets and glaciers?
- How do ice cores taken from different places compare to one another?
- Can they build upon existing data by studying an earlier, or later, time in the ice record?

Sometimes they need more ice samples because they're asking questions they didn't know to ask or couldn't answer before. As new technology is developed, scientists have better methods for testing the ice cores. Or scientists from other fields, like chemistry or microbiology, might have their own questions.

Scientists also consider whether an ice sheet or glacier is in danger of melting, which would mean they need to retrieve cores sooner than later. Sometimes, scientists are too late. In 2018, an international team visited the Grand Combin Glacier on the border of Switzerland and Italy and found what they believed to be a good spot to drill. But by the time they made it back for the actual drilling—just two years later—the glacier ice was no longer solid enough to drill because of **freeze-thaw**. Other drill sites, including ones on glaciers on Kilimanjaro, in Indonesia, and in the Andes, have completely disappeared over the last twenty years. Some ancient ice now only exists in the form of ice cores stored in freezers like the one at The Ohio State University.

After scientists narrow down the information they're looking for, the next step is to scout out a specific location to drill. They might visit the ice sheet or glacier and look for an area where the ice is thick and the **bedrock** is flat. (Flat bedrock means less deformation of the ice.) They use ground-penetrating radar to look for the ideal spot and will often drill a shallow core to test the ice's consistency and see what data it contains. This scouting-out process may take a field season or more to complete.

Once scientists return home from scouting, they must write a grant proposal. A grant proposal is a formal request for money to conduct the full research expedition. They write about why they want to drill, why it's important, where they will drill, who they'll take on the trip, the equipment they'll need, and how much it'll cost. Ice core expeditions are very expensive. They can cost from a few million dollars to over fifty million dollars! So much goes into transporting the team and their equipment to the location and then getting the ice cores safely back to a lab for testing. Ice core scientists send their proposals to the National Science Foundation and private organizations that fund scientific research. It can take six or more months to find out if a proposal has been approved.

Even ice cores were not immune to the effects of COVID-19. The pandemic put a pause on most scientific research trips, including ice core retrievals.

A cargo ship delivers and picks up supplies and equipment at McMurdo Station in Antarctica.

Field Season

A field (or drill) season is the period of time when scientists are working in the field. In the field means on location or away from the laboratory. Because extreme winter weather conditions make things dangerous and difficult, scientists and their teams visit ice sheets and glaciers during the summer months. This makes it a little bit easier to get to the location and safer to work there.

In Antarctica, the field season is from late October to mid-February. In Greenland, it's from April to July or August. In the low latitudes (tropical regions), the field seasons vary a bit, but they are typically from May to September.

Why is it summer in Antarctica when it's winter in the Northern Hemisphere? Seasons are reversed in the two hemispheres because the planet is titled toward the sun at opposite times of the year.

The National Science Foundation

The National Science Foundation, or NSF, is a federal agency that was created by Congress in 1950. Its goal is "to promote the progress of science; to advance the national heath, prosperity, and welfare; to secure the national defense; and for other purposes." That's a fancy way of saying it works to support scientific research with the goal of learning and understanding more about the world.

The NSF uses part of its budget to fulfill grants for researchers at American colleges and universities across a wide variety of STEM (science, technology, engineering, and mathematics) fields. It also helps provide money for research equipment, such as telescopes and specialized computers, and research sites. For example, the NSF funds the National Ice Core Facility (NSF-ICF) in Colorado. It also funds McMurdo Station, which is the largest research station in Antarctica.

GETTING THERE

Even after a proposal has been approved, it can take a year—and often longer—to coordinate the expedition. Ice core teams range from a handful of people to groups of fifty or more. And while being in the field can be a fun adventure, no one is going along because they want a vacation. Everybody has a job to do and must be willing to pitch in whenever and wherever they're needed.

In addition to paleoclimatologists or other scientists, a team includes mechanics, engineers, drillers, field assistants, truck and tractor drivers, cooks, and medical staff. To get these people to the chosen location, the team needs **porters** and **sherpas** to help guide them and carry supplies (if they're working in the mountains), airplane or helicopter pilots, interpreters to communicate with the local people, and so on.

As you can probably imagine, they also need a lot of stuff! It's not unusual for an expedition team to use five or six **tons** (yes, *tons*) of equipment and supplies. These supplies can include special extreme-weather tents for sleeping, eating, and lab work; warm clothing and protective gear like sunglasses; lab tools; tractors; snowmobiles; sleds; lights; generators; batteries; computers; drills and drill fluid; table saws and handsaws to cut the ice once it's above the surface; and other equipment to test the ice cores in the field and supplies to store the ice cores so they can be safely transported back to the lab. And since they're working remotely, teams also need basics like fuel, meals and snacks, pots and pans, clothing, medicine and first aid supplies, portable bathrooms, and toilet paper—*phew!* You get the idea.

When it's possible, ice core teams will use equipment that's been stored on location from previous expeditions. For example, there are places to store vehicles and other large equipment at McMurdo Station and multiple stations in Greenland. But most of the time, team leaders need to get everything and everyone to the drilling location by chartered airplanes, helicopters, ships, or some combination of modes of transportation.

Getting a team to the top of a mountain or ice sheet requires behind-the-scenes helpers, too. Scientists and researchers who *aren't* going might help organize, pack, and catalog supplies to go through **customs** in foreign airports. Or they might make sure that the drills are working. Everyone has the same goal: to successfully retrieve and bring back ice cores that can tell us about ancient climates, our current climate, and our future climate.

An ice core expedition isn't a quick, easy trip. But once everyone and everything is on location and set up, it's time to experience the thrill—and challenges—of the drill!

See *if you can solve*

How many things do you think you use or need during a typical day? Make a prediction, and then keep a running list. Include *everything*, even things like toilet paper and a glass for water. Estimate how much each of these items weighs (or actually weigh them) and then add up how heavy your daily supplies would be.

If you travel by boat from the tip of South America to the tip of the Antarctic Peninsula, your journey takes about two days. If you travel by plane, the trip is two hours. I wonder how long it would take if you swim, though.

Skibirds

To get in and out of Antarctica and Greenland, ice core teams often take special military cargo planes, such as a C-17 Globemaster 3 or an LC-130 Hercules. The LC-130, nicknamed Skibird, can hold 45,000 pounds of equipment and supplies. It lands on a runway made of gravel or smooth ice, with gear that looks like—you guessed it—large skis.

Skibirds are flown by pilots from the New York Air Guard's 109th Airlift Wing. The pilots practice takeoffs and landings on snow and ice during the summer on the Greenland Ice Sheet at a station called Raven Camp.

A neat thing about Skibirds is that they have a JATO (aka RATO) system. JATO stands for Jet-Assisted Takeoff (RATO stands for Rocket-Assisted Takeoff). Essentially, this a system of four small rockets attached to each side of the plane between the wings and tail that can help the aircraft become airborne. They need this assist because the low air pressure in high altitudes makes traditional takeoff challenging.

An LC-130 (or Skibird) dropping off passengers at the
Amundsen-Scott South Pole Station.

COOL VOCABULARY
(in order of appearance)

Arctic Circle: the latitude line that goes around Earth at approximately 60° 33' 39" N, creating an imaginary circle at the top of Earth's sphere.

elevation: how high something is compared to sea level.

axis: an imaginary straight line that a planet (or object) turns around when it rotates.

parallel: describes lines that are always the same distance apart and never touch. For example, railroad tracks are parallel. So are the rungs of a ladder.

plateau: a flat landform that is elevated from surrounding areas on at least one side.

gigaton: a unit of mass equal to one billion metric tons, or 2.2 trillion pounds.

monsoon: a seasonal change in the direction of the strongest winds in a region. These weather patterns cause heavy rainfalls, high temperatures, and damaging winds.

Tibet: a region in Central Asia that covers most of the Tibetan Plateau. It's often called the Roof of the World because of its high elevations.

endemic species: species of plants or animals that are only found in a particular geographic area. In other words, they don't exist or grow naturally anywhere else in the world.

zooplankton: animal organisms that drift in oceans.

expedition: a journey or trip taken by a group for a particular purpose, especially for science or research.

freeze-thaw: the repeated, back-and-forth process of ice melting and refreezing as temperatures change.

bedrock: the solid rock under ice or other surface materials.

porter: a skilled mountain guide who helps set up the camp and carry equipment. The terms porter and sherpa (or Sherpa) are often used interchangeably.

sherpa: a skilled mountain guide who manages the safety of a climbing group. (The word Sherpa, with a capital S, refers to a member of an ethnic group that lives in the Himalayan Mountains, whose members often work as mountain guides.)

ton: a unit of weight equal to 2,000 pounds.

customs: the authority in charge of unloading and admitting goods brought into a country.

SCIENCE IN ACTION: INSTANT ICE

Glaciers and ice sheets take a long time to form. But you can make "instant ice" using supercooled water. (Remember supercooled water from Part I? That's water below the freezing temperature but not yet in a solid state.)

WHAT YOU'LL NEED

A large bucket or bowl
5 pounds of ice cubes
Water
Table salt (Rock salt
   will also work.)
A long-handled spoon
A thermometer

A plastic bottle of unopened,
   purified water, at room
   temperature

NOTE: Tap water *won't* work for this experiment. Also, make sure the bottle is plastic, not glass.

WHAT TO DO

1) Fill your bucket or bowl about halfway with ice cubes.

2) Add just enough water (this can be from your sink) to the bucket so that your ice cubes can move around a little. You don't want them to float to the top, though.

3) Add 1 cup of salt to the ice/water solution and stir with the long-handled spoon. Attach the thermometer to the edge of the bucket.

4) Let your solution sit until it's 25 degrees Fahrenheit (-3 degrees Celsius). If it's not getting to 25 degrees, try adding another ½ cup of salt, mixing, and letting it sit a while longer.

5) Once the ice/water solution is at 25 degrees, place the sealed bottle in the middle of the ice. You want the ice to surround the bottle. (The top of the bottle can stick out a little, though.)

Let it sit in the ice water until the temperature of the solution is between 20 and 15 degrees Fahrenheit (between -6 and -9 degrees Celsius). This will probably take an hour or so. Keep an eye on the experiment. Don't let the water in the plastic bottle freeze. If it does, let it thaw before starting over from the beginning. Ideally, you want the temperature to be below 20 degrees Fahrenheit. The colder you can get everything, the better.

6) Carefully remove the plastic water bottle from the bucket. Firmly tap or hit the counter or table with the bottle. Ice crystals should begin to spread inside the bottle. Instant ice!

7) If it doesn't work, try putting the bottle back into the bucket and cooling it for 30 minutes longer, or adding more salt. Be patient, it can take a few tries.

WHAT'S HAPPENING?

Ice crystals need something to grow on. When you bang the bottle on the counter, the jarring causes some of the water molecules to line up into a crystal lattice (a type of 3D structure of atoms) and—ta-da!—a surface for ice to grow on.

PART III

HOW DO SCIENTISTS RETRIEVE ICE CORES?

Yay! We've made it! After plenty of planning and traveling, we've arrived at the drilling site. If we're not staying at a station, the first thing we need to do is set up camp.

Ice core teams use tents built for extreme weather. They are made from waterproof fabric and can withstand high winds. (Don't forget, the winds in Antarctica can blow up to 200 miles per hour.) These tents come in a variety of sizes and shapes. Many are pyramid-shaped, **geodesic domes**, or half-cylinder-shaped. Each tent sleeps a few people. There is typically a larger tent or structure where the whole team can come together for meetings or meals.

You can see a Scott tent (the pyramid-shaped one in the back) as well as a snow-block wall to help block the wind at this training camp ("Snow School") at McMurdo Station in Antarctica.

When a team is working on a mountain, the camp setup might be a little different. Teams typically set up a base camp lower on the mountain, getting there by truck, snowmobile, horseback, or a combination of modes of transportation, depending on the area. When they're ready to drill, the team travels to the drill site on foot, using **crampons**, trekking poles designed for ice and snow, and other mountaineering tools. Teams often set up tents around the borehole to help protect them from the cold wind and harsh sun.

When doing deep ice core drilling, scientists sometimes also dig a **trench** or a snow cave near the borehole. It may seem strange, but working in a trench or snow cave is actually warmer than working at ground level, since you don't have to deal with wind. The snow also offers some insulation from the cold. Consider this: Would you rather be outside on a very cold day with or without wind? Why? How cold the wind makes you *feel* is known as the wind chill. The wind chill in polar regions and at high altitudes causes your lungs to ache and stings any exposed skin.

Going to the Bathroom Out in the Field

If ice core teams don't have a portable bathroom—sometimes jokingly referred to as a polar potty—they typically have a "poop tent" near their camp. There, team members leave waste in buckets lined with disposable plastic bags. The waste is eventually carried out for proper disposal when the expedition is over.

 And yes, if you're wondering, the poop and pee freeze.

When they are working in the field and not near a bathroom tent or an enclosed outhouse, scientists might use a makeshift outhouse built with blocks of snow! These structures often have only three walls, enough to block out wind and give some limited privacy. If nothing else is available (or if they just don't want to go outside in the middle of the night to walk to the tent), ice core team members use pee bottles. These are designated bottles that store urine to protect the environment. (Human waste has micro-organisms that release greenhouse gases if it's left untreated!)

See if you can solve

The pyramid-shaped tents used in polar areas are called Scott tents. They have an inner wall made with a material that doesn't allow condensation to form. (Condensation is the water droplets that form on a cold surface when it's humid.) Scott tents are named after British polar explorer Sir Robert Falcon Scott, who, in 1912, attempted to become the first person to reach the South Pole. He and his team were beaten by another explorer, Roald Amundsen, and his team by just under five weeks. Sadly, Scott and his companions froze to death while waiting out a blizzard on their return home.

What kind of tent would you design to use in extreme weather? Think about how big it would be and what features it could have that might help during high winds or cold temperatures. Draw and label your tent. What would it be called?

The Big Red Bus

When scientists and other support staff arrive in Antarctica, they need a way to get from the icy airfield to McMurdo Station. It's Ivan the Terra Bus to the rescue! Ivan is a famous red-and-white transport bus that's been around since 1993. And just like the continent where it works, Ivan is big.

The terra bus (terra means land, or earth) is over 46 feet (14 meters) long, 12 feet (3 meters) wide, and 14 feet (4 meters) tall. Its six tires are each 6 feet (1.8 meters) in diameter and 2 feet (.6 meters) wide. Ivan can hold up to fifty-six passengers along with their personal gear.

THE DRILLS

Once camp is set up, it's finally ice core time! Ice cores are retrieved from ice sheets and glaciers using drills. Not the drills you might find in your garage or tool shed, though. There are two types of tools commonly used: hand augers and mechanical drills.

Scientists use hand augers when they want a sample of ice that's up to a hundred feet (30 meters) deep. An auger is a simple tool that has a barrel and a drill head. The drill head for an auger used in ice has several stainless steel or carbide (another type of metal) "teeth." Around the barrel is a spiraling piece of metal. Have you ever noticed the winding piece of metal wrapping around and up a screw? This is called a helix. When you turn a screw, with a screwdriver or an electric drill, the screw cuts into the wood or other material. Often, you'll see sawdust or tiny bits of the material come to the surface. This is because the helix is moving the sawdust up and out of the hole.

A screw is solid, but an auger used to cut ice cores has a hollow barrel. As the auger is turned downward, the drill head cuts the ice and a core is stored in the barrel while the chips of ice (also called cuttings) move up and out of the hole via the helix.

Hand augers are usually turned by hand using what's called a T-bar handle. Which, you've probably guessed, looks like a capital letter T. Once the ice core is drilled, the auger is pulled up and out of the ground so the scientist can take the ice core out of the barrel. It takes at least two people to use this system.

For ice samples over 100 feet (30 meters) deep, scientists use mechanical drills run by fuel-powered generators. This type of drill is anywhere from 3 to 20 feet (1 to 6 meters) long and 2 to 5 inches (5 to 12 centimeters) in diameter. The drill is suspended over the borehole by a **pulley** system using a cable. The cable holds the sonde (the part of the drill that goes into the borehole) and powers the **drill head**. The sonde consists of the drill head; an outside barrel, which doesn't move; and an inside barrel, which has a helix that turns. Like the middle of a hand ice auger, this barrel is hollow to hold the ice core sample. A sonde also typically has an anti-torque system. This is a set of blades that pushes out from the outer barrel and grips the ice to hold the drill in place as the inner barrel rotates. Without one, the entire drill would spin and it wouldn't be able to cut the ice.

At the end of a drill is either an electromechanical or an electrothermal drill head. The first type of drill

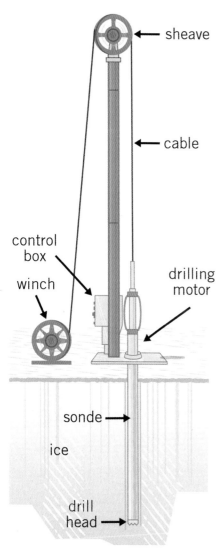

sheave

cable

control box

winch

drilling motor

sonde →

ice

drill head →

head uses a motor to turn a ring of metal teeth that cut the ice into an annulus, or ring. (The center part of the ring is the ice core.) The second type of drill head uses a metal ring heated by electricity to melt part of the ice as it moves downward. Both types of drills also have special chambers within the barrel where either the ice cuttings or meltwater are stored until the drill is pulled up.

A close-up of a mechanical drill head.

A close-up of one type of thermal drill head. Because the ice is melted, ice cores drilled using a thermal drill head are clear.

The drill head is chosen based on the condition, thickness, and temperature of the ice and the depth to which you are drilling. For example, electrothermal drill heads are usually used for "warm ice"—meaning ice that's above 14 degrees Fahrenheit (-10 degrees Celsius), which is more common in tropical or low-latitude glaciers.

Who knew ice could be "warm"?

Ice deeper than 100 feet (30 meters) or so also needs a thermal drill head, because an electromechanical one would put too much pressure on the ice. Often, a combination of the drills is used to retrieve a core. Scientists might use an electromechanical drill head when they begin drilling, because the top layers of ice can withstand that. Then they might switch to an electrothermal drill as they drill deeper, because the lower ice layers are more likely to crack.

A scientist holds up an ice core section taken from a glacier in Antarctica.

DRILL FLUID

Have you ever made homemade Popsicles? Imagine you use a plastic straw as the Popsicle stick. What happens to the straw when the Popsicle is frozen? It freezes and gets stuck inside the Popsicle. Something similar would happen if scientists drilled an ice core and didn't use drill fluid.

Scientists need to keep the borehole open while they're working. But they also need to keep the drill from getting stuck down there. Glacier ice is under a lot of pressure, more pressure the deeper you go, and that pressure can cause the ice to shift and trap the drill. Or the meltwater displaced by an electrothermal drill head can re-freeze, causing the drill to become stuck that way. So scientists pour fluid into the borehole to protect the drill and the hole itself. Fluid is used when teams drill deeper than about 1,900 feet (600 meters), although it's occasionally used at shallower depths, too. It depends on the ice.

Drill fluid used in cold environments must have certain prop-erties. For example, it needs to be close to the density of the ice, be inert (in other words, it won't react to other things like water, air, etc.), be nonflammable, and be safe for the environment. In the past, drill fluids were made of harsh chemicals that were left behind when scientists were done drilling. Today, teams typically use a mixture of food-grade ethanol, water, and a chemical solution that increases density. Ethanol is a liquid made from corn and nat-ural sugarcane. It's what's in alcoholic drinks such as beer and wine, and things like vanilla extract. Besides being safe for people, ethanol eventually evaporates, making it better for the environment, since it won't stay in the hole forever.

Solar Power to the Rescue

One of the challenges Dr. Lonnie Thompson and his team faced when they retrieved the first tropical ice core (from the Quelccaya Ice Cap in Peru in 1983) was powering their drill. Climbing to the top of a mountain with heavy fuel for the generators to run the drill was going to be too hard for the horses. The scientists came up with an impressive solution: they designed the first solar-powered drill.

The system had over a few dozen panels, which the team laid out in the sun to collect power. The panels were easier and lighter to carry up to the drill spot than a generator, but they had to be moved to stay in the light. And that took time. Today, scientists use more technologically advanced panels that can be rolled up into a lightweight bundle.

Before Dr. Thompson and his team used the new solar-powered drill, they had to test it. They did this by setting up the solar panels and drill on the roof of a garage at The Ohio State University. Then, suspending the drill off the edge of the roof, they drilled into blocks of ice placed on the ground. It worked!

THE THRILL OF THE DRILL

Ice cores aren't drilled in one go. That would require a *really* long drill. Instead, ice cores are gathered section by section by running the drill in cycles, or drill runs. A drill run consists of these steps:

- The drill is lowered into the borehole.
- An ice core is drilled. These sections of ice are usually between 3 and 20 feet (1 and 6 meters) long. The length depends on how long the drill barrel is.
- The drill is pulled back to the surface.
- The ice core is carefully removed from the drill's barrel.
- The drill is prepared and then sent back into the borehole.

Ice core teams can drill approximately 3 to 5 meters of ice in one hour. This means it can take three to five days to cut an ice core that's a few hundred feet (90 meters) long. If time in the field is limited, the drill is run twenty-four hours a day, in shifts. Deeper ice cores are frequently cut over the course of several field seasons.

The step where scientists remove an ice core from the drill's barrel takes extra cooperation. If the drill (or hand auger) is light enough, one or two people may be able to hold the drill and push the ice core out from the top, while another person guides the core out of the bottom of the drill. If the drill is too heavy, cranes or pulley systems lift the sonde vertically and then lay it horizontally on supports. Someone uses a pole to push the ice through and out from the inner barrel.

After each drill run, the sections of ice are processed. Preliminary data, such as its length, diameter, and temperature,

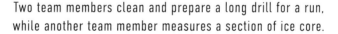
Two team members clean and prepare a long drill for a run,
while another team member measures a section of ice core.

are recorded and logged. Afterward, the ice is cut into 3-foot (1-meter) pieces using a table saw. Once the pieces of ice are ready, scientists place them in plastic sleeves (also known as **polybags**), or sometimes plastic netting, and label the sample. The ice cores' next stop may be a snow cave, where they will have time to get used to the atmosphere above Earth's surface.

A snow cave is a great place to store ice cores while they wait to be shipped back.

Snow caves have air ducts cut into them to help circulate air and keep the inside cold. Occasionally, ice cores are left to acclimate until a later field season. But if the ice core is going to a lab right away, scientists put the bagged or netted sections inside insulated cylinder containers with lids and labels. Each lab has a different way of labeling the ice segments, but they typically include the location, the year, and the ice core's segment number.

Ice cores will stay frozen up to 32 degrees Fahrenheit (0 degrees Celsius), but if the temperature is above 0 degrees Fahrenheit (-18 degrees Celsius), the gases that are trapped in the tiny air bubbles inside the core will begin to diffuse, or spread out. This means the atmospheric data can be lost. So, even though it may seem strange, scientists often bring portable freezers with them on ice core expeditions to use for storage until it's time to ship samples back or to keep cryo-packs cold. Cryo-packs are ice packs that are made with special gel that stays colder longer than regular ice.

When the time comes to ship ice cores back to laboratories, scientists remove them from the freezer (or snow cave) and place them in sturdy, insulated containers or in special cardboard boxes. The boxes are insulated with a layer of **spray foam**. Each box holds six cylinder containers. Cryo-packs are placed around the tubes. Once the boxes are packed, they are loaded onto animals to carry down the mountain or loaded into vehicles, typically cargo trucks.

An example of an insulated box used to transport ice cores. The blue packets are cryo-packs. The black foam under the cryo-packs is used to cover the contents before the box is sealed up.

A yak can carry two boxes of ice cores down a mountain or across a glacier.

Scientists often make an agreement with the country that they're retrieving samples from. In return for a country's help and cooperation, teams set aside a portion of the ice core for the country to use for its own research. But if ice cores don't need to be set aside (or if the host country has already received its ice), the boxes are put on cargo planes and flown back to the laboratory or university where the expedition originated. To protect the ice from melting, the plane flies "cold deck," meaning it doesn't turn on the heat, and it flies above 10,000 feet (3,000 meters), where the air is colder. Portable freezers might also be plugged into the plane to transport samples.

Because they are usually coming from out of the country, ice cores go through customs at the international airport they're flying into. From there, the ice cores are loaded into refrigerated semitrucks and taken to the university or lab.

Ice as Art

Ancient ice is fascinating from a scientific viewpoint, but it's also beautiful. Digging holes out in the field gives scientists a close-up view of the ice layers in their various shades of brilliant blue and other colors. Wanting to share the beauty and also get people to think about climate change, a California-based artist named Peggy Weil created a film called *88 Cores*. In this four-and-a-half-hour video, she spliced together digital photos of ice cores taken from the Greenland Ice Sheet that had been drilled in the late 1980s and early 1990s. The film, along with still shots of the ice cores, had its first exhibit in December 2017 at the Climate Museum in New York City. The film was continuously played on a screen in a room, and people could stop and watch as over 110,000 years of ancient ice panned up. Museum visitors probably felt as if they were taking a time-traveling elevator down to bedrock.

See if you can solve

NASA is working on sending astronauts to Mars someday. But did you know that they've also put together a group of scientists and engineers (another type of problem solver) to figure out how to drill ice cores from our neighboring red planet?

Mars used to have water on its surface, but based on recent observations, it doesn't anymore. At least not in the way we think of liquid water here on Earth. Water molecules exist on Mars inside its rocks and beneath the planet's surface, and there is ice in its polar regions. But the ice is a combination of H_2O ice and CO_2 ice, or what we call **dry ice**. Scientists aren't sure what caused this change. They hope to be able to drill a Mars ice core and study it someday.

What are some of the problems or challenges you can think of that NASA and scientists will have to figure out before drilling ice cores on Mars? Do you have any ideas for solving these challenges?

THE CHALLENGES OF DRILLING

As interesting as drilling ice cores can be, it isn't fast work. Or easy. First, there's the weather. Working in extreme weather conditions can mean that scientists have to deal with unexpected storms, bone-numbing cold, and winds strong enough to knock them over. They could be stuck inside their tents for days, even weeks, waiting for a break in the weather to safely drill.

The temperatures are also tiring. Think about a time when you played out in the snow or cold weather. Maybe you went sledding or skiing. You were probably ready to fall into bed by the end of the day. Now imagine what it would be like to be in the cold and working hard for days or weeks on end. Working in the cold drains your energy, making you tire faster than you normally would. This can lead to exhaustion, which can then lead to mistakes. That could be costly to data or to the health and safety of an ice core team. The repetitive nature of the work might also cause team members to lose focus.

Being on a mountain in the tropics isn't any easier. Along with changing temperatures, avalanches, sunburn, and possible hiking injuries, the high altitude is a serious challenge due to thin air. As scientists and other team members climb higher above sea level, the barometric pressure (the pressure of the air) drops. This means the air is less dense than it is at sea level or lower down a mountain. And this decrease in density causes a decrease in the concentration of oxygen in the air. At sea level, the concentration of air that is oxygen is roughly 21 percent. But at 22,000 feet (6,700 meters) above sea level, as the glaciers are on the Huascarán mountain in Peru, the oxygen concentration level is only 9 percent!

Nine percent—that takes my breath away!

Any elevation over 8,000 feet (2,400 meters) above sea level is considered high altitude. People who live in these areas become adapted to thin air. But if scientists aren't used to it, their bodies need time to adjust or they could become ill with altitude sickness. This can lead to trouble breathing, headaches, dizziness, nausea, and, in some cases, death. The higher someone goes, the more dangerous it becomes. This is why climbers and ice core team members working at extremely high altitudes often need to bring canisters of oxygen with them.

Storms, injuries, and illnesses aren't the only things that can delay an expedition. Even with lots of planning and care, drills and other important equipment can break down. Or they can become stuck inside the borehole because of the pressure of the surrounding ice. And it may take several hours or even days to figure out how to remove them. Even under the best of conditions, meaning that the weather and the equipment cooperate, scientists might not be able to drill all the cores they'd like because sometimes, something else goes wrong—the dreaded exploding ice core.

Ice sheets and glaciers are dense. There is *a lot* of pressure on the bubbles of air inside ice, and that can cause problems. Have you ever been swimming or diving and noticed that your eardrums felt pressure, or hurt a little? This happens because water has a different pressure than air. The deeper you go, the more pressure there is on your eardrums and the more your ears hurt.

Ice is similar. The older the ice (and the deeper scientists drill), the more pressure there is. Once expedition teams get past around 1,900 feet (600 meters) down, the pressure can become too great. Every once in a while, when the ice core is pulled up to the surface and experiences the difference in pressure, it—*craaaack!*—breaks. Or worse, shatters.

This, of course, is disappointing for scientists who have worked so hard and traveled so far. Sometimes, they can collect data by putting the pieces back together like a broken glass or vase. Other times, that section of the ice core is useless. The scientists simply have a gap in their record of the climate. But if they get enough information about the climate from the ice that came after that missing section, they can still make good inferences, or educated guesses.

Another concern for scientists is working with local people to ensure that they are comfortable with the expedition. This is especially true when working in tropical areas or the Third Pole. For many indigenous tribes in these areas, the mountains and the glaciers on them are sacred. They are, understandably, not happy about outsiders drilling into them. Expedition teams must ask permission ahead of time and let local tribes and leaders know what they're doing and why.

See if you can solve

Ice core team members pack a few personal items to help them feel more comfortable while in the field, especially if they're staying for a while. These items might include pictures of family and friends, board games to play during downtime, movies to watch, books, musical instruments, cameras, and journals. What would you take?

KEEPING WARM IN THE FIELD

Working in freezing temperatures is dangerous. Even when collecting tropical ice cores and low-latitude ice cores, the temperatures can fall below 0 degrees Fahrenheit (-18 degrees Celsius). Scientists working in these conditions have gear designed for extreme cold weather—called ECW gear—which includes water-resistant and wind-resistant pants, parkas (typically brightly colored so they're easily seen in the snow), hats or balaclavas, ski masks, gloves, and sunglasses or goggles. Because the sun reflects off the snow and ice, sunscreen is also essential in the field.

What's black and white and red all over? A sunburned penguin!

Layers like thermal underwear or fleece liners also help protect scientists in the cold. First, they trap tiny pockets of air that then act as insulation. (Air doesn't allow heat to move around well, so it's a good insulator.) And second, layers can be added or removed when necessary. For example, if a team member is moving around a lot, they're going to get warmer and might need to take off a layer. It's important not to sweat too much in cold weather because when cold air hits the sweat, it causes the sweat to evaporate quickly, which makes them feel chilled. Then their body has to work harder to keep warm. Losing too much body heat can cause **frostbite** or **hypothermia**. To maintain a safe and comfortable temperature inside their tents or temporary buildings, team members use heaters run by generators. A generator is a machine that uses gas (or other fuel sources, like solar power) to create electricity.

If you work as a team member at a US research station in Antarctica, you are issued a Big Red and a pair of Bunny Boots. A Big Red is a Canada goose–down parka that can withstand -100 degrees Fahrenheit (-73 degrees Celsius). Bunny Boots are heavy white rubber boots that have pockets of air and layers of wool insulation inside to keep your feet warm and dry. They get their name because they kind of look like the large feet of an arctic hare.

One of the first things scientists and other researchers do when they arrive for work in Antarctica is go to Survival School, also known as Happy Camper School or Snow School. During this overnight training, they learn how to protect themselves in their new setting. Lesson plans might feature: how to build a wind barrier outside a tent, how to tie knots, how to keep clothes dry, how to use a two-way radio, and how to avoid crevasses and other dangers.

Blue Ice and Drilling . . . Sideways?

Glaciers and icebergs usually look white because there is a blanket of snow covering them. But when high winds blow the snow off or it's otherwise worn away, and something (like mountains) block the ice from moving, older ice is exposed. Over millions of years, the air bubbles in this old ice have been squeezed out. This means the ice is very dense. And blue! To understand why, you first have to know that light travels in waves and these **wavelengths** appear to us as color. Longer light wavelengths, like red and yellow, are quickly absorbed by the dense ice, while the shorter light wavelengths, like blue, are reflected. Blue ice is so dense that it absorbs every color except for blue.

Blue ice occurs in many areas of the world, including a small region of Antarctica. Called a blue-ice area, the winds there are so strong that any new snowfall gets blown away. The ice covers the rocky ridges of the landscape underneath and stops at the nearby mountains. These rocky ridges also push older ice up, closer to the surface. As a result, the ice core record is accumulated horizontally, rather than vertically. Think of it like pouring syrup on waffles. The syrup (the ice) fills the pockets (the rocky ridges) but then flows out over them and across the whole waffle (the region). Now put your hand or another barrier (the mountains) on the edge of the waffle. When the syrup reaches it, both the previously poured and newly poured syrup pile up.

In 2010, a team of scientists from Princeton University drilled a horizontal ice core in the Allan Hills (a group of hills in East Antarctica). They ran out of time before they could get to bedrock, so they returned in 2015. On this trip, they reached bedrock and retrieved an ice core estimated to be 2.7 million years old! This is the oldest ice drilled to date. Teams hope to return to the area for even older ice someday soon.

Another cool thing about blue ice is that these regions seem to attract meteorites, including some from Mars. Scientists aren't sure why, but they think the katabatic winds help carry the pieces of meteorites to the area, where they get caught in rocks and sand. So far, more than 45,000 meteorites have been found in Antarctica. NASA even has a treasure map of sorts for scientists to use when meteorite hunting.

A meteor sits on top of blue ice in Antarctica. Because it's so dense, blue ice is often used as an aircraft runway.

Let's Hear It for the Chef!

The human body has to work harder to stay warm when it's cold. Hard work = more calories burned. Scientists and other support team members out in the field can burn up to 5,000 calories a day! For reference, that's more than twice the number of calories an average twelve-year-old needs. All that extra hard work means that ice core teams need a lot of food.

Whether someone is working at a research station or in a more remote field site, expedition meals are planned in advance. After all, if the team runs out of something, they can't just go to the grocery store. Most of the food is dried, canned, or (surprise!) frozen. Fresh fruit and vegetables are called freshies. They're not always available, since it's difficult to fly them in before they go bad. Some research stations grow plants **hydroponically**, but the **Antarctic Treaty** doesn't allow soil from other places on the continent. This is to protect the native ecosystem.

Food on an expedition is more than just fuel. Mealtimes are also an opportunity for team members to connect with one another. And because climate science is collaborative, team members are often from different countries. Meals are a place where they can share foods, languages, and their cultures. Having an expert chef on-site can make a huge difference in field morale. Stop for a moment, and pretend you're a scientist who's been out in the field all day. You're cold from head to toe, exhausted and achy. On top of that, you're so hungry you'd probably eat just about anything. And then you make it back to base camp, sit down with friends, and find homemade cinnamon buns, breads, cookies, brownies, pasta, tacos, hamburgers, fried chicken, and pizza waiting for you. You feel better, right?

Some stations, like this one at the South Pole, use hydroponic gardens to grow fresh vegetables.

I'd feel better with a fish taco.

Research stations have large, modern kitchens that can feed the larger groups who work in Greenland and Antarctica during their summer months. Base camps that are farther away, like those on mountains in the tropical areas, use outdoor grills or camp stoves. Because waste must be carried out when team members leave, leftovers are turned into new meals.

If there isn't a camp cook, that might mean weeks of simple sandwiches, canned foods, or MREs. MRE stands for Meal, Ready-to-Eat. They are individual packets of meals that can be heated up. Team members might take turns preparing meals for the whole group as well.

Snacks are important, too. But if you want to enjoy a piece of candy or a protein bar out in the field, you'd better have strong teeth, because these foods will freeze! To avoid this, team members tuck candy bars *inside* their coats and clothes, next to their bodies.

See if you can solve

Because they are surrounded by frozen water, ice core team members take advantage of their environment and melt snow and ice to get drinking and cooking water. They don't often use the water to bathe, though. It takes a lot of fuel to melt ice, and being hydrated is a bigger priority than being clean. Out in the field, scientists clean themselves using water and a washcloth, or body wipes. At some stations, team members are allowed to take three-minute showers every second or third day. Limiting bathing times can really help save water. This might be true where you live, too.

Consider this: the average low-flow household showerhead uses 2.5 gallons (9.5 liters) of water a minute. So if you took a three-minute shower, you'd use only 7.5 gallons of water. (2.5 x 3 = 7.5)

How long are your showers? (If you don't know, set a timer.) Using the estimate of 2.5 gallons a minute, figure out how much water you typically use. Brainstorm some ways you can save water. (And no, you probably can't convince your grown-ups to let you give up bathing!)

Referred to as The Sauna, this tent is where scientists in the field can wash up using hot water and a washcloth.

The First All-Female Team in Antarctica

Women study and drill glaciers and ice sheets all over the world. This hasn't always been the case, though. It might surprise you to hear that many people used to believe women shouldn't be in science and other STEM fields, let alone researching on the harshest continent in the world. People believed the **stereotype** that women weren't smart enough or physically strong enough, and that they would be a distraction to male researchers. For a long time, the US Navy, which used to transport people to Antarctica, wouldn't take women there.

During the 1969–1970 drilling season, six women made history as the first all-female team in Antarctica. The group included four women from the Byrd Polar and Climate Research Center (then called the Institute of Polar Studies): Dr. Lois M. Jones (the team leader and geochemist), Kay L. Lindsay (an entomologist), Eileen McSaveney (a geologist), and Terry Lee Tickhill (the team's field assistant and cook). The remaining team members were Pamela Young (a research assistant from New Zealand) and Jean Pearson (a journalist). The group did research in the Dry Valleys and quickly proved that women are just as capable as men when it comes to surviving the coldest, windiest, and driest place on Earth. While there, the team also became the first women to reach the South Pole by plane. So that no one person would be the "first," the six women stepped off the plane's ramp together.

COOL VOCABULARY
(in order of appearance)

geodesic dome: a rounded structure with polygonal (multisided) panels. A geodesic dome resembles one half of a soccer ball.

crampon: a traction device that attaches to footwear and has spikes that help prevent slipping on the ice.

trench: a deep ditch or cut in the ground. Trenches used in ice drilling can be upwards of 30 feet (9 meters) deep.

pulley or pulley system: a simple machine that uses a wheel to turn a cord, rope, or belt on its rim in order to move objects.

drill head: the part of a drill that cuts or melts the ice.

polybag: a clear, thick plastic bag made from polyethylene.

spray foam: a chemical product made with two materials that expands and creates an airtight layer.

dry ice: solid carbon dioxide. It's used to keep food or medicine frozen. It can also be used to create special effects, like fog.

frostbite: an injury caused when your skin and its underlying tissues freeze. Frostbite can result in amputation of the affected area.

hypothermia: a condition of dangerously low body temperature, when your body loses heat faster than it can make it. Hypothermia can cause confusion, fatigue, uncontrolled muscle movement, and even death.

wavelength: the distance between light waves.

hydroponically: a way of growing plants without soil, using a water- and nutrient-based solution.

Antarctic Treaty: an agreement that ensures the freedom of scientific research on the continent of Antarctica and that no country can claim Antarctica as their own or use it for military purposes. Because Antarctica has no indigenous population, fifty-four countries (as of 2020) have signed the Antarctic Treaty.

stereotype: a widely held and unfair assumption about a group of people.

SCIENCE IN ACTION: CREATING A HYDROPONIC GARDEN

The soil in Antarctica isn't good for growing things. It doesn't have the nutrients plants need. Because bringing in soil from other places is not allowed in Antarctica, some stations grow food hydroponically. You can do this at home, too.

WHAT YOU'LL NEED

Scissors
An empty 2-liter plastic bottle
An old cotton T-shirt
Distilled water
A measuring spoon
Plant food, like Miracle-Gro
A mixing bowl

Duct tape
Coconut coir, found at plant nurseries
Vegetable or herb seeds
Aluminum foil
Optional: perlite, found at plant nurseries

WHAT TO DO

1) Use the scissors to carefully cut off the top $\frac{1}{3}$ of the plastic bottle.

2) Cut or tear the T-shirt into two strips, approximately 10 inches long and 1 to 2 inches wide. (An old towel also works well.) Lay one strip on top of the other. Next, tie a knot at the bottom to connect the two strips. This will be your wick.

3) Turn over the top part of the bottle you cut off so that it resembles a funnel. Thread the wick through the small hole so that the knot stays above the hole. If the knot can slip through, tie a bigger knot.

4) Next, use the distilled water, measuring spoon, and plant food to mix nutrient-rich water in a bowl. You can make extra for later, but it should be used within 10 days. Otherwise, it loses its potency.

5) Place the funnel-like part of the bottle inside the bottom part of the bottle. You can use some duct tape to help keep it in place. This will be your grow area.

6) Break up the coconut coir according to the package directions. Add ⅓ cup of perlite if you'd like. This is what will hold your seeds and plants. Add the coconut coir to the grow area. Make sure to put the knot in the middle of the coconut coir.

7) Pour the nutrient-rich water over the coconut coir and into the bottom of the bottle. The water should touch the bottom of the grow area.

8) Add a few seeds to the growing area and cover with more coconut coir.

9) Wrap a strip of foil around the garden system. This step isn't necessary, but it will help keep algae from growing in your water.

10) Place your hydroponic garden in a sunny window and wait. Check to make sure the coconut coir stays moist and add water to the reservoir as needed. In a week or two, you should have a small plant!

WHAT'S HAPPENING?

Like the soil in Antarctica, the coconut coir and perlite have no nutrients. The mixture of plant food and water provides the nutrients your plants need.

Because water is usually captured and reused in larger hydroponic systems, this form of gardening uses less water. How else might hydroponic gardening help us deal with climate change?

PART IV

WHAT CAN ICE CORES TELL US ABOUT CLIMATE CHANGE?

LEARNING about past climates and figuring out how to use that information is kind of like putting together a jigsaw puzzle. The puzzle is huge and has pieces scattered around the world. Some of the pieces are really old and hard to get to. It would be impossible for one person, one university, or even one country to collect them all. This is why scientists across the world are working on their own section of the puzzle while also working together to address climate change by sharing the information found in each section.

But what exactly are scientists looking for when they study ice cores, and what does this information mean? Let's find out what happens once ice cores are retrieved, boxed up, and sent back to laboratories. It's time to take a peek into these frozen time capsules.

THE NSF-ICF

For some ice cores, the first stop is the National Science Foundation Ice Core Facility in Lakewood, Colorado. The NSF-ICF is like a warehouse-sized library of ice. The main freezer is kept at -32 degrees Fahrenheit (-36 degrees Celsius), and it contains more than 72,000 feet (22,000 meters) of ice cores. That's roughly the height of two and a half Mount Everests stacked on top of each other! Ice cores are examined in a separate area, which is kept at -4 degrees Fahrenheit (-20 degrees Celsius). The facility also includes a clean room. A clean room is an area designed to keep out any particles that may contaminate a sample. The room has special air filtering systems to control the dust, temperature, and other things that might damage an ice core, and has strict rules. For example, scientists working in a clean room might have to wear sterile gloves, or the number of people allowed to work in there at the same time might be limited. Universities and research centers studying ice cores have storage freezers, cold work areas, and clean rooms, too.

The extreme cold inside these cold work areas can cause problems. For example, the ink inside pens might freeze, or batteries and other electrical equipment might run out of energy more quickly or even stop working.

At the NSF-ICF, ice cores go through a system of ten stations. This is called a core processing line, or CPL. But whether it's at the NSF-ICF or in a university lab like the Byrd Polar and Climate Research Center, the process for analyzing ice cores is similar. The order and number of steps, the equipment used, and what is being analyzed will be a bit different, though. Just like ice cores themselves, labs are unique.

Below is the process that the NSF-ICF follows.

FIRST THINGS FIRST

First up: a lot of sitting around. To allow ice cores to acclimate to the new environment, scientists leave them inside the freezer, still packed in the plastic, tubes, and boxes they were transported in. How long they stay in the freezer depends on factors like how much ice was retrieved, how old the ice is, and where it was retrieved.

Boxes of ice cores wait in the storage freezer at the National Science Foundation Ice Core Facility.

STATION 1: UNPACKING

The ice cores eventually get unpacked and laid on a long metal bench. Scientists check each one to see how it handled the travel. They look for any visible features, such as a crack or **debris** trapped inside when the ice froze. The ice core is carefully measured and entered into a database.

At NSF-ICF, researchers use pencils to mark where the ice cores will be cut and to draw arrows distinguishing the younger ice from the older ice. (The tip of the arrow points to the younger end of the ice.) In other labs, the ice is simply labeled "top" (younger ice) and "bottom" (older ice) on the correct ends. Ice cores are physical timelines of past climates. If the direction of the ice cores were accidentally reversed, the timeline wouldn't be correct.

Pencil lead doesn't hurt the ice. Pencils contain graphite, a type of carbon. And even when scientists are testing for carbon, they can decontaminate the ice beforehand. Permanent markers aren't used because the ink can soak into the ice crystals.

STATION 2: HORIZONTAL SAW

Using a table saw, scientists level out the top of the ice and then cut the core horizontally in the middle. (It's kind of like how you'd slice a baguette in half to make a sandwich.) Next, the sample is cut into pieces of various sizes. Each university or research lab decides its own cutting pattern. If you look at the pattern used at the NSF-ICF, it might remind you of a window with multiple, different-sized panes.

The size of each piece is **predetermined** based on how much ice is needed for a particular test or analysis. At the NSF-ICF, roughly half of the ice is used for testing isotopes, chemistry,

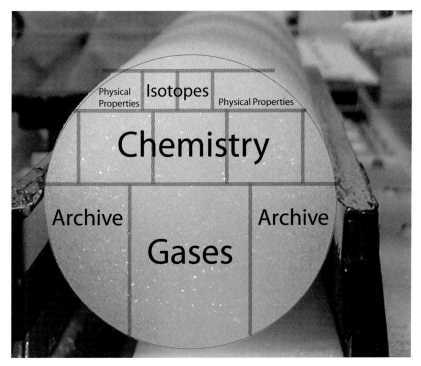

The cut plan used at the NSF-ICF ice core processing line.

and atmospheric gases. The other half is examined for physical properties and photographed before being archived, meaning put into storage and saved for later.

Some labs, like the Byrd Polar and Climate Research Center, use a band saw to cut ice cores. A band saw has a long, skinny blade that runs vertically and takes up less room than a table saw.

After the ice has been divided into pieces, some of it is sent on to Station 5. The remaining ice is analyzed at Stations 3 and 4.

Heads up! Before reading about those stations, it would be helpful to check out the Pardon the Interruption box on the following page.

Pardon the interruption, *but here are some things you need to know about chemistry when it comes to ice cores.*

To understand what scientists are looking for inside ice cores, you first need to understand atoms. Atoms are the tiny building blocks that make up everything in the universe. They're kind of like LEGOs in that they fit together with other atoms to create matter. (Remember, matter is anything that takes up space and has weight. For example, oxygen and other gases, dust and rocks, water, clothes, cars, computers, books, you!) But atoms aren't the tiniest LEGO pieces . . . They are made up of even smaller particles called electrons, protons, and neutrons. And get this: atoms can share, give away, or steal electrons. They're kind of like toddlers with toys that way. An ion is an atom or group of atoms that's either positively or negatively charged, thanks to those exchanged electrons.

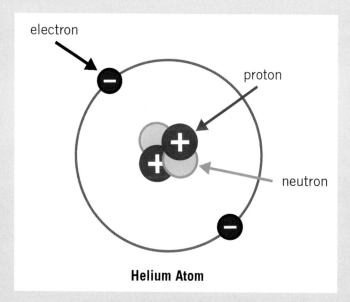

Helium Atom

Chemistry is the branch of science that studies these interactions. And when we talk about chemistry, we talk a lot about elements. An element is a substance made up of only one kind of atom. There are 118 known elements, including oxygen, iron, helium, gold, and silicon. You might have seen something called a periodic table of elements. This is a collection of the known elements and their symbols. For instance, the symbol for oxygen is O.

Compounds are a combination of elements, such as water. Water contains two hydrogen (H) atoms and one oxygen (O) atom. When you're thirsty on a hot day, you're really looking for a glass of ice-cold H_2O.

Paleoclimatologists check for elements, compounds, and other things trapped inside an ice core because those things tell us what was in the region's atmosphere and environment when that layer of ice was created.

STATION 3: CHEMISTRY

Scientists analyze ice cores for traces of more than forty elements. For example, they look for carbon, which can tell them if there was a forest fire near the ice, and sodium, which tells them there's sea salt in the ice. Elements like lead and mercury tell scientists how much pollution was in the atmosphere at the time.

To look for chemicals inside ice cores, scientists use instruments known as a mass spectrometer and a Coulter counter. A mass spectrometer measures the change in the weight and charge (called the mass-to-charge **ratio**) of atoms or molecules that have gone through a magnetic or electric field inside the instrument. A Coulter counter works by measuring a sample's electrical resistance. (In other words, how much does it resist an electrical current?) Since scientists already know the electrical resistance of certain atoms and molecules, they can use the information from this test to determine what's in the sample.

STATION 4: ISOTOPES

Isotopes are atoms of the same element that have different masses. They are kind of like Oreos. Even though some have one layer of cream filling and others have two (or even three) layers of cream filling, they're all still Oreos. Only, instead of different numbers of cream layers, isotopes have different numbers of neutrons!

Two of the most important isotopes that scientists look for when analyzing ice cores are oxygen and hydrogen. These are found inside the ice's water molecules.

First up, oxygen.

There are two common types of oxygen isotopes: heavy and light. (They have different numbers of neutrons and therefore different masses.) Scientists compare the ratio of these two oxygens inside an ice core to the standard oxygen ratio in ocean water. But how does *that* help scientists learn about *temperature*?

When something is light, it takes less energy to move it. On the flip side, when something is heavy, it takes more energy to move it. The energy needed to move isotopes during the **water cycle** comes from the sun. So when scientists find a higher ratio of heavy oxygen isotopes in polar areas, they know the global temperatures were warmer.

Next up, hydrogen.

Like oxygen, hydrogen comes in both heavy and light versions. After figuring out the hydrogen isotope ratio, scientists then compare the data to what they found when they looked at the light-to-heavy oxygen ratio. This gives them a way to check their math, since the results should be similar.

To determine oxygen and hydrogen ratios inside ice cores, scientists might use a mass spectrometer, a Coulter counter, or a

An ice core being cut on a planer at the NSF-ICF processing line.

Picarro. A Picarro is an instrument that uses light waves to determine what's inside the sample.

STATION 5: PLANER

If the ice isn't going to Stations 3 and 4 for testing, it moves on to Station 5. Here, scientists use a **planer** with a (very sharp!) carbon steel metal blade to smooth out a large area of ice. Smoothing out the ice's surface makes it easier for scientists to study the core at the next few stations. Scientists may also use a ceramic knife to smooth out the smaller areas of the core that the planer didn't get. Ceramic knives are made of zirconium dioxide, a hard and very tough material that won't damage the ice.

STATION 6: CONDUCTIVITY

Conductivity is the degree to which something can carry and move electricity. A conductor is a material that transfers electricity. For example, electricity can move easily through most metals, but wood and plastic aren't good conductors.

Ice made with water from a faucet is also not a good conductor. This is because it's been treated (made safe for us to use) so the atoms inside don't have much **acidity**. But glaciers are formed out of precipitation from the sky. There are volcanic ash,

CO_2, and sulfuric or nitric **acid** in the atmosphere, which make rain and snow acidic. Higher acidity means higher conductivity.

To test conductivity at the NSF-ICF, scientists use the electrical conductivity method, or ECM. They place two electrodes on top of a leveled sample. (An electrode is a conductor through which electricity can enter or leave an object.) Next, they slide the electrodes across the ice. As the electrodes move, a current is sent from one to the other. Instruments measure how easily the electricity passes through the ice.

The strength of this electrical current tells the scientists the levels of acidity in the layers of the core. Since higher temperatures cause chemical reactions to happen faster, higher conductivity indicates summer (or warmer) seasons in the layers of ice. Lower conductivity indicates winter (or colder) seasons.

STATION 7: IMAGING

At this station, scientists use special equipment to photograph each sample and get a **high-resolution image**. They want to be able to see and count the individual season layers of ice, document any cracks or fractures, and zoom in on the tiny air bubbles that hold atmospheric gases. Having the ice go through the planer first makes it easier to get a sharper image.

The main reason scientists take pictures of the ice is to have a permanent record of what it looked like. Sections of ice cores will be sent to outside laboratories for various types of tests. Unfortunately, during many testing procedures, the ice has to be destroyed. But the information ice cores hold is valuable enough to make that sacrifice.

Maybe in the future, scientists will be able to test ice cores without having to melt or crush them.

STATION 8: PHYSICAL PROPERTIES

At this station, scientists study the ice on a **light table**. They want to make sure they are observing and recording every physical detail, and the light makes it easier to see things like dust and the seasonal layers inside the ice. These seasonal layers, or bands, vary in appearance. They can be thin or thick, and usually look light or dark gray, or different shades of green or brown. Their characteristics depend on how much snow accumulated that year, what happened in the atmosphere, where the ice was formed, and from what depth it was drilled.

Next, scientists move to a special illumination system. They cut a wafer-thin piece of ice and place it under a high-powered microscope. This system magnifies the ice so scientists can study the internal structures of the ice crystals. The individual crystals have various thicknesses and can be pointed in different directions. These characteristics show up as various colors and pointed shapes on a computer screen that's connected to the microscope. The images might remind you of looking through a kaleidoscope. They're pretty but also useful. Learning how the ice crystals are oriented (what direction they're pointing toward) can tell scientists how the ice flowed in the past and how it might flow in the future.

Another tool scientists at the NSF-ICF use to capture detailed images of ice cores is a hyperspectral camera. This type of camera can take pictures across light spectrums, including ones we can see with our eyes and ones we can't see, such as **infrared** and **ultraviolet**. Being able to see ice cores across the light spectrum helps scientists to identify what the minerals are in the dust trapped inside ice. Hyperspectral technology is new, and hopefully it'll be useful to paleoclimatologists in other ways, too, in the future!

STATION 9: ATMOSPHERIC GASES

Something special is trapped inside the tiny bubbles of ice cores: ancient air. There's no other place in the world where ancient air can be found; it's one of the unique things about icy time capsules. The contents of this air can tell scientists a lot about the climate at the time. At this station, they look for and measure atmospheric gases such as carbon dioxide, nitrous oxide, and methane.

Carbon dioxide levels are important because they are directly related to temperature. Carbon dioxide, or CO_2, is like the temperature control button for Earth's thermostat. When CO_2 levels go up, so do temperatures.

 CO_2 is a compound made up of one carbon and two oxygen atoms.

Using polar ice cores and other proxy data, scientists have been able to estimate the CO_2 levels of the planet over the last 400,000 years. For most of that time, CO_2 levels stayed within a range from 180 **parts per million (ppm)** to around 300 parts per million. This was normal and predictable.

However, a shift began around the start of the **Industrial Age**, and over the last 250 years, CO_2 levels have jumped to 420 ppm—the highest level ever recorded. Humans are adding more CO_2 than the planet and natural processes (like photosynthesis) can take out. Because CO_2 levels and temperatures are related, our global temperatures have also risen at an average rate of .14 degrees Fahrenheit (.08 degrees Celsius) every decade since the late 1800s. This rate of warming is only getting faster. It is neither normal nor predictable.

Methane and nitrous oxide are other greenhouses gases that

scientists might measure. Methane levels are important because methane absorbs and traps much more heat from the sun's rays than carbon dioxide does. And nitrous oxide is important because it can have a strong effect on the environment. After it's released (mainly through fossil fuel use and agriculture emissions), it stays in the atmosphere even longer and raises temperatures at a higher rate than carbon dioxide does—over 300 times faster!

To extract atmospheric gases from ice core bubbles, scientists crush the ice, grate it, or melt it in special system. One of these is called a Continuous Ice Core Melter System. With this type of equipment, scientists place an ice core (or a section of an ice core) inside a chamber. And since scientists want to know what's in the ancient air and not the air in the laboratory, this chamber is **vacuum-sealed**. One end of the ice is set on a plate that heats up. The meltwater goes into the test vials. It is then directed to other instruments (such as a mass spectrometer or **spectrophotometer**) that measure gases and other chemical elements of the ice core.

Another instrument scientists use to evaluate the atmospheric gases is a gas chromatographer. It works by heating a sample (ice core meltwater in this case) and inert gas inside a

A Continuous Ice Core Melter System melts part of an ice core.

tube until they **vaporize**. (An inert gas is a gas that doesn't react to or cause changes to the substance it's combined with.) This tube is inside a temperature-controlled oven that splits the sample into its different components and allows them to exit the oven at different speeds. A **detector** identifies those speeds. And since the scientists know which components travel at what speed, they can determine what's in the sample.

A gas chromatography mass spectrometer, or GC-MS, might be used as well. This instrument combines mass spectrometry and chromatography to analyze gases.

STATION 10: PACK UP

After scientists are done studying the ice core, they pack up what's left of it. Each remaining sample is placed inside a poly-bag, labeled, and put into a storage tube. Sometimes, an ice core is divided into multiple pieces—and placed in multiple bags—for storage. Ice is then saved inside a freezer for future use.

See if you can solve

Parts per million (ppm) is basically a percentage (for example, 25 per-cent or 50 percent of something) involving much smaller numbers. It's useful when discussing tiny amounts, or concentrations, of something that can make a huge difference. For example, pollution or a poisonous substance. If you're having a hard time imagining something small hav-ing a big effect, try this experiment.

Fill an 8-ounce glass with water. Next, squeeze one drop of food col-oring into the water and stir with a spoon. What happens? Try adding a drop of food coloring to a 16-ounce glass of water and observe.

How much water do you need for that one drop of food coloring to not make a noticeable difference?

OTHER WAYS SCIENTISTS DATE ICE

In Part I, we learned that scientists count the layers inside ice cores to determine how old the ice is, or to date it. There are a few other ways scientists can figure out this information when the layers aren't clearly defined.

For example, scientists can count the layers by testing the ice core's electrical conductivity. Remember what we just learned about the electrical conductivity of ice cores? Summer (warmer) months show up as high conductivity. Winter (colder) months show up as low conductivity. Using this information, scientists can count the number of years or layers. One summer section plus one winter section would equal one year.

Scientists studying ice from Greenland and Antarctica can also tell the seasons apart based on differences in the ice's chemistry. These places are surrounded by sea ice in the winter, and that sea ice helps keep components from the ocean (like salts and acids) from getting into the atmosphere and mixing with the snow. When it's warmer and the sea ice melts, scientists start to see more oceanic chemicals in the layers of the ice core.

Historic events are yet another way scientists can date ice. If there is a record of an event, researchers can link the ice to that era. For instance, because of global testing and use of nuclear weapons from 1945 through the 1980s, an element called plutonium can be found in ice cores from those years. Other historical events, like volcanoes, show up in ice cores, too. Take the 1991 eruption of Mount Pinatubo in the Philippines. Since scientists know exactly when and where the volcano erupted, they can pinpoint that layer in the ice from that area. Using it as a reference, they can figure out the age of the ice.

A tephra (volcanic ash) layer inside an ice core. This type of layer can help scientists date the ice. This layer is from a volcanic event that occurred 3,200 years ago off the Antarctic Peninsula.

And here's something interesting: the COVID-19 pandemic will also show up in ice cores! When countries all over the world encouraged citizens to stay home to try to contain the virus, there was less traffic, and as a result, less air pollution. Those changes will be visible to scientists when ice cores from 2020 are drilled in the future.

Viruses and Pathogens

Isotopes, atmospheric gases, and debris aren't the only things found inside ice cores. For example, in 2021, American and Chinese scientists working together found twenty-eight previously unknown viruses that were 15,000 years old. (The ice samples had been drilled from the Guliya ice cap in China in 2015.) And in 2022, French scientists found dozens of new viruses in permafrost in Siberia, including one that was 48,500 years old!

Are these viruses and other **pathogens** dangerous to us? It's possible. In 2016, there was an outbreak of anthrax (a serious infectious disease) in the Russian Arctic. Thousands of reindeer and almost a hundred people were infected. Scientists believe it was caused by the melting of the permafrost, which released spores that had been frozen inside an infected, dead animal. This is another reason why scientists use great care when retrieving and studying ice cores.

 These are nicknamed zombie viruses because they're still infectious after being frozen.

Yep. It's Humans.

Earth has natural climate cycles, and many variables affect temperatures. But scientists know for a fact that humans are significantly contributing to climate change. The telltale clue? Carbon dioxide.

Like oxygen and hydrogen, carbon comes in different weights. And these different weights come from different natural sources. Some carbon comes from plant matter. Some comes from volcanic gases. And some comes from **organic matter**.

Scientists know that the increase in CO_2 isn't coming from carbon found in organic matter or volcanic remnants because the ratios between these two carbons has been decreasing. Plus, carbon from organic matter decays relatively quickly. It's not found in matter older than 50,000 years.

The only thing left *and* old enough to release carbon is plant matter. Fossil fuels and oils are made from decomposing plants and animals that eat those plants. And they are way older than 50,000 years. So scientists can confidently conclude that burning them is the reason for the increase of carbon dioxide in our atmosphere.

CLIMATE MODELS

The best way to predict the future is to look at the past. Every bit of data that scientists gather from ice cores might be part of the solution to climate change. Using the information they have, they create a climate prediction model.

If you've ever watched a weather forecast, you've probably heard a meteorologist use the term weather models. These models predict what the weather will be like in the next day, or week, or couple of weeks. Weather models are computer programs that use data like wind speed and direction, temperature, air pressure, and precipitation, and turn that information into a likely forecast.

Climate models, on the other hand, predict what our climate might look like decades, or even hundreds or thousands of years, from now. Like weather models, climate models use data—only there's much more data. These programs use complex mathematical equations that are based on the laws of physics, or, in other words, the facts we know about how nature works. Supercomputers process the data to give us simulations, or models of what might happen, based on the historical information.

Supercomputers aren't like your home computer. They are a single computer or a group of connected computers that are extremely powerful. They have a lot of memory and are capable of calculating a tremendous amount of data at high speed. And instead of taking up a corner of a desk, they can fill the space of a school gym or a warehouse. There are dozens of supercomputer systems that help scientists across the world predict current weather and climate change patterns. One of them is used by the National Oceanic and Atmospheric Administration, or NOAA.

It's called the Weather and Climate Operational Supercomputer System. This system is able to process quadrillions (yes, quadrillions!) of calculations every second.

Quadrillion is a number represented by a 1 followed by fifteen 0s. To put it in perspective, one million is represented by a 1 followed by six 0s, and there are one thousand million millions in a quadrillion.

The real challenge in predicting future climates is that there are so many factors to consider. Scientists have to look at many different systems: atmosphere (air), hydrosphere (oceans), cryosphere (ice), lithosphere (land surfaces), and biosphere (living organisms). Not only do they have to understand and predict how each of these systems will respond in the future, but they also have to consider how the systems will interact with one another. And they're constantly changing! No wonder it can take thousands and thousands of pages of computer **code** to run a climate model.

Huh, you may be wondering. *If it's so hard to work with the variables that go into climate, how can we believe what the models are telling us about climate change?* Excellent question! The answer is: scientists can test the models by plugging in old data and seeing if the result matches real history. If a program can "predict the past" and tell us what happened, weather- or climate-wise, then we can be fairly confident that it is accurately predicting the future, too.

Now, meteorologists don't always get the weather prediction right. And there's a possibility that climate models might be a little off, too. For example, maybe a glacier will disappear in 500 years, instead of 400 years as predicted. But small variations like this are unimportant when looking at the big picture. Our planet's climate is changing in a way that affects all living things.

WHAT DO SCIENTISTS DO WITH THIS INFORMATION ABOUT OUR FUTURE?

Many of the events that climate models predicted are already happening. We can see them every day, all around us. There are more heat waves, bringing higher temperatures and lasting longer, than there were in the past. These are especially dangerous for areas that aren't equipped to handle them. We're also seeing higher temperatures in places we don't expect. For example, in 2020, the Siberia region—an area *inside the Arctic Circle*—recorded 100 degrees Fahrenheit (38 degrees Celsius). That's never happened before.

Higher temperatures also mean we're experiencing more frequent and stronger hurricanes, longer droughts, devastating wildfires, the disappearance of sea ice, the retreat of glaciers, the flooding of coastal areas, and the migration of animals to cooler areas. If we don't act now, some climate models show global temperatures up by an average of 5 to 10 degrees Fahrenheit by the end of the century.

But there's hope.

That's right. No panicking! Be chill, like me.

Countries are beginning to listen to scientists. In 2015, more than 190 leaders from countries from all over the world signed the Paris Agreement. In this treaty, countries agreed to work together to decrease greenhouse emissions and take other steps to limit global warming to just 2.7 degrees Fahrenheit (1.5 degrees Celsius) by 2100. This would hopefully keep some of the predicted effects of climate change—coral reefs dying off, and coastlines and small islands becoming uninhabitable—from happening.

The treaty also requires countries to be held accountable. For example, the United States has pledged to come up with low-carbon power sources by 2035. Several countries, including Canada, Japan, the United Kingdom, South Korea, and the United States, have promised to cut *all* greenhouse gas emissions made by humans by 2050. The balance between creating and removing greenhouse gases is called net zero.

On a smaller scale, states, provinces, and other territories have also committed to reducing greenhouse gases. California is working to have net-zero carbon dioxide emissions by 2045, and British Columbia (a province in Canada) has a plan to reduce their greenhouse gas emissions to 80 percent below 2007 levels by 2050.

Many companies have started using more climate-friendly, **sustainable** practices. They're using less plastic and packaging, working to become **carbon neutral**, manufacturing goods with recycled materials, creating or using machines that produce less carbon dioxide, and donating to organizations working to address climate change.

Young people are working to improve the climate, too. In 2015, Xiuhtezcatl "X" Martinez, an indigenous activist from America, spoke to the United Nations General Assembly on Climate Change. He was fifteen at the time and addressed the leaders of the world in three languages! In 2016, sisters Ella and Amy Meek, then ten and twelve years old, started Kids Against Plastic in the United Kingdom. That same year, teenagers Nikita Shulga and Sofiia-Khrystyna Borysiuk cofounded the Kompola project. This project helps schools in Ukraine reduce waste by providing compost stations. And you've probably heard of Sweden's Greta Thunberg. In 2018, when she was fifteen years old, Greta decided to put pressure on her country's leaders to meet their carbon emission targets. She did so by skipping school for 251 Fridays while holding a sign that read: SCHOOL **STRIKE** FOR CLIMATE. Other students in Sweden and around the world began holding school strikes and protests to demand change. Also in 2018, eighteen-year-old Lesein Mutunkei from Kenya founded Trees4Goals, which aimed to plant eleven trees for every soccer goal he made to combat **deforestation**. There are so many other young people speaking up, standing up, and making a difference.

WE'VE COME A LONG WAY ... AND WE HAVE A LONG WAY TO GO

At the beginning of this book, you stood in front of a freezer door. After talking about what ice cores are, how they are made, and where they can be found, we put on our pretend coats and gloves. We braved extreme weather and traveled far. In our imaginations, we've been to the top of mountains and to the bottom of the world. And while we were there, we retrieved miles and miles of ice, carefully sent it back to labs, and analyzed it in numerous ways, before packing it up for safekeeping in subzero freezers.

Ice cores are challenging to retrieve but beautiful to look at and fascinating to study. And ice cores are unique. Like nothing else on Earth, they are time capsules that hold frozen water, atmosphere, and debris from thousands and even millions of years ago. It's important to preserve them for the same reason we create other types of time capsules: protecting and understanding the past can help us protect and understand the future.

Ice cores can tell us a lot about climate change. Addressing this important and complicated global emergency might feel impossible. How can one person, a group of people, or even a whole world of scientists working together possibly make a difference? Where do we start?

As the saying goes: Snowflakes are one of nature's most fragile things, but just look what they can do when they stick together.

COOL VOCABULARY
(in order of appearance)

debris: scattered bits of material that have been broken down. Inside ice cores, this may include rocks, plant fossils, dust, and dirt.

predetermined: decided on ahead of time.

ratio: a comparison of two (or more) numbers of the same kind. For example, you could use a ratio to compare the number of kids to adults in your family, or the number of blue fish to red fish in an aquarium.

water cycle: the process in which all water moves around Earth in different states of matter (liquid, solid, and gas).

planer: an electric-powered machine or handheld tool used to cut material into a consistent thickness to create smooth, flat surfaces.

acidity: the level of acid in a substance.

acid: a chemical with high levels of hydrogen ions. This is measured with the pH scale. Acid is common in things we eat; for example: oranges, lemons, pineapples, vinegar, carbonated drinks.

high-resolution image: a photograph or other image that shows something in fine detail.

light table: a table or tilted surface with glass or translucent plastic on top and a light source below.

infrared: an energy wave that has a frequency below red light. We use infrared waves every day in things like remote controls and the infrared lamps that restaurants use to keep food warm.

ultraviolet: an energy wave that has a frequency below violet (blue) light. Ultraviolet rays cannot be seen by human eyes, but they are what cause sunburns and make black-light posters glow.

parts per million (ppm): how many units of one thing are in one million units of another thing.

Industrial Age: a time period roughly from 1760 to 1840 when the process of manufacturing goods went from small shops to large-scale factories. Things like steam power, electricity, railroads, and gas-powered vehicles changed how and where people lived.

vacuum-seal: to remove the air inside a closed chamber before securely closing the chamber.

spectrophotometer: an instrument that measures the intensity of light that's absorbed.

vaporize: to turn from a liquid into a gas.

detector: a device or process that identifies something.

pathogen: any organism (such as a virus, bacteria, or microorganism) that can cause disease.

organic matter: any matter from a living or dead animal or plant. Organic matter can contain plants, but plant matter only contains plant materials.

code: a series of instructions or directions that tell a computer how to do a task. Codes use special languages unique to computers.

sustainable: able to meet present-day needs without hurting future people.

carbon neutral: having achieved a balance between the amount of CO_2 humans produce and what we (or nature) remove.

strike: the refusal to work or attend other required events (like school) in order to protest an injustice or pressure a higher power to act.

deforestation: the clearing out of a wide area of trees.

SCIENCE IN ACTION: OBSERVING CARBON DIOXIDE AND A LEAF CREATING OXYGEN

Humans breathe out carbon dioxide. Plants and trees absorb that CO_2 and turn it into oxygen. Here are two ways to observe these processes separately.

EXPERIMENT 1
WHAT YOU'LL NEED

A small red cabbage

Water

A pan

A stove

2 small glass jars or glasses

A measuring cup

A drinking straw

An adult, for supervision

Optional: a sieve

WHAT TO DO

1) Shred the red cabbage or pull off several leaves. With adult assistance, place it in 2 cups of water in the pan on the stove for 10 minutes. The water should turn a purplish blue. Let the cabbage juice cool, then remove the leaves. (You might have to pour it through a sieve.)

2) Pour ¼ cup of the cabbage juice into each small jar.

3) Set one jar aside. This is your control sample.

4) Place the straw in the second jar of juice and gently blow for several minutes. Observe what happens. (The water should turn from purplish blue to a lighter shade of purple or pink.)

WHAT'S HAPPENING?

In this experiment, the red cabbage juice acts as a pH indicator. When the CO_2 from your breath dissolves in the test water, it causes an acidic reaction and changes the color of the water. The color of the juice in the control glass stays the same.

EXPERIMENT 2
WHAT YOU'LL NEED

A clear plastic or glass cup
Water
A freshly cut green leaf
A window

WHAT TO DO

1) Fill your cup with water and let it sit until the water is at room temperature.
2) Submerge the leaf in the water. (It's okay if a little bit of the stem sticks out.)
3) Place the jar by a sunny window and wait for a couple of hours.
4) Come back to your jar and observe any changes. You should see tiny bubbles on the leaf and jar.

WHAT'S HAPPENING?

The bubbles are oxygen. They were created when the plant went through photosynthesis, the process by which it uses the sun's energy to create its own food.

ACKNOWLEDGMENTS

I'd like to give a special thank-you to the following experts, who went above and beyond in sharing their time and expertise: Drs. Ellen Mosley-Thompson and Lonnie Thompson, Dr. Stacy Porter, and Richard Nunn. I would also like to express my deep gratitude to all the people who shared photos to use in this book. I appreciate your generosity and passion, as I'm sure young readers will.

This book wouldn't be possible without the help of so many other "snowflakes" who've stuck with me, including my amazing editor, Sally Morgridge; agent extraordinaire Marie Lamba; and my favorite cheerleaders, Christina Farley, Andrea Mack, and Debbie Ridpath Ohi. And, of course, I wouldn't be able to do what I do without my family: Jim, Matt, Rachel, Sam, Meg, and Abigail; my parents, Darrell and Carol; my mother-in-law, Marian; and everyone else who shows up at our large family gatherings. Thank you all for your love and support.

SOURCES

Adler, Ben. "IPCC: Window to avert catastrophic climate change quickly closing." Yahoo News, 2022. https://www.yahoo.com/news/ipcc-window-to-avert-catastrophic-climate-change-is-quickly-closing-161926811.html.

Alley, Richard B. *The Two-Mile Time Machine: Ice Cores, Abrupt Climate Change, and Our Future*. Princeton University Press, 2014.

Arenschield, Laura. "15,000-year-old viruses discovered in Tibetan glacier ice." Ohio State News, 2021. https://byrd.osu.edu/news/15000-year-old-viruses-discovered-tibetan-glacier-ice.

Bruckner, Monica. "Paleoclimatology: How Can We Infer Past Climates?" last modified 2022. Montana State University, https://serc.carleton.edu/microbelife/topics/proxies/paleoclimate.html.

Carbon Brief. "How do climate models work?" 2018. https://www.carbonbrief.org/qa-how-do-climate-models-work/.

Cimons, Marelene. "The First Women in Antarctica." National Science Foundation, 2010. https://beta.nsf.gov/news/first-women-antarctica.

Compound Interest. "The science of ice cores: Atmospheric time machines." 2017. https://www.compoundchem.com/2017/08/15/ice-cores/.

Davies, Bethan. "Ice core basics." Antarctic-Glaciers.org, 2020. https://www.antarctic-glaciers.org/glaciers-and-climate/ice-cores/ice-core-basics/.

Garrison, Cassandra, Clare Baldwin, Marco Hernandez. "Scientists scramble to harvest ice cores as glaciers melt." Reuters, 2021. https://www.reuters.com/graphics/CLIMATE-CHANGE/ICE-CORES/zjvqkjkjlvx/.

Greenfieldboyce, Nell. "Scientist Have Found Some Truly Ancient Ice, But Now They Want Ice That's Even Older." NPR, 2020. https://www.npr.org/2020/12/26/949159524/scientists-have-found-some-truly-ancient-ice-but-now-they-want-ice-thats-even-older.

Harvilla, Beth. "Ohio State scientists seek funds to preserve rare ice core collection." *The Columbus Dispatch*, 2020. https://www.dispatch.com/story/news/2020/11/13/ohio-state-scientists-seek-funds-preserve-rare-ice-core-archive-climate-change/6247005002/.

Hickey, Hannah and Taguchi, Kiyomi. "NSF-funded deep ice core to be drilled at Hercules Dome, Antarctica." UW News, 2020. https://www.washington.edu/news/2020/12/08/hercules-dome-ice-core/.

Lindsey, Rebecca. "How do we know the build-up of carbon dioxide in the atmosphere is caused by humans?" NOAA Climate.gov, 2022. https://www.climate.gov/news-features/climate-qa/how-do-we-know-build-carbon-dioxide-atmosphere-caused-humans.

Moens, Jonathan. "Andes Meltdown: New Insights into Rapidly Retreating Glaciers." *YaleEnvironment360*, 2020. https://e360.yale.edu/features/andes-meltdown-new-insights-into-rapidly-retreating-glaciers.

National Science Foundation Ice Core Facility. "About Ice Cores," undated. https://icecores.org/about-ice-cores.

National Snow and Ice Data Center. "Glaciers," undated. https://nsidc.org/learn/parts-cryosphere/glaciers.

National Snow and Ice Data Center. "What is an ice sheet?" undated. https://nsidc.org/learn/parts-cryosphere/ice-sheets.

OSU.EDU. "Researchers capture oldest ice core ever drilled outside the polar regions." 2017. https://news.osu.edu/researchers-capture-oldest-ice-core-ever-drilled-outside-the-polar-regions/.

Romano Young, Karen. *Antarctica: The Melting Continent*. What On Earth Books, 2022.

SciJinks. "How do snowflakes form?" undated. https://scijinks.gov/snowflakes/.

Stoller-Conrad, Jessica. "Core questions: An introduction to ice cores." NASA, 2017. https://climate.nasa.gov/news/2616/core-questions-an-introduction-to-ice-cores/.

Time Scavengers. "Proxy Data: What are proxy data?" undated. https://timescavengers.blog/introductory-material/what-is-paleoclimatology/proxy-data/.

Vince, Gaia. "The century of climate migration: why we need to plan for the great upheaval." The Guardian, 2022. https://www.theguardian.com/news/2022/aug/18/century-climate-crisis-migration-why-we-need-plan-great-upheaval#:~:text=Climate%2Ddriven%20movement%20of%20people,become%20greater%20and%20more%20urgent.

World Wildlife Federation. "Six ways loss of Arctic ice impacts everyone," undated. https://www.worldwildlife.org/pages/six-ways-loss-of-arctic-ice-impacts-everyone.

VIDEOS

Asia Scotland Institute, 2021, "The Third Pole: How climate change is affecting the Tibetan Plateau." https://www.youtube.com/watch?v=_VtkUIxf4Bw.

NOVA, original air date 2/5/2022, "Polar Extremes." https://www.pbs.org/wgbh/nova/video/polar-extremes/.

PBS, 2017, "How do glaciers move?" https://www.youtube.com/watch?v=RnlPrdMoQ1Y.

PBS, "How Ice Cores Prove Climate Change Is Real," 2019. https://www.youtube.com/watch?v=myxVsYI4WZk.

PBS News Hour, 2021, "Glacier ice samples act as records of climate change's impact on Earth." https://www.pbs.org/newshour/show/glacier-ice-samples-act-as-records-of-climate-changes-impact-on-earth.

PBS/NOVA, 2020, "What Do You Eat in Antarctica?" https://www.pbs.org/wgbh/nova/video/what-eat-antarctica/.

University of Maine, 2011, "How do ice cores allow researchers to look at global climate change?" https://www.youtube.com/watch?v=iC-TH8pV0Cc.

US Ice Drilling, 2013, "Ice Core Processing: Discovering Earth's Climate History." https://www.youtube.com/watch?v=gESJSAXsL0Q.

Voice of America, 2018, "Ice Core Drilling." https://www.youtube.com/watch?v=fHWno Gl79y4.

INTERVIEWS

All communications are emails with author unless otherwise noted.

Porter, Stacy (Assistant Professor of Environmental Science at Wittenberg University), December 27, 2021.

Porter, Stacy, January 21, 2022.

MacAyeal, Douglas R. (Professor of Geophysical Sciences at University of Chicago), Zoom interview with author, March 16, 2022.

MacAyeal, Douglas R., March 16, 2022.

Porter, Stacy, March 20, 2022.

Mosley-Thompson, Ellen (Distinguished University Professor of Geography [Atmospheric Science], The Ohio State University, Senior Research Scientist at the Byrd Polar and Climate Research Center), in-person conversation with author, March 22, 2022.

Thompson, Lonnie (Distinguished University Professor of Earth Sciences at The Ohio State University, Senior Research Scientist at the Byrd Polar and Climate Research Center), in-person conversation with author, March 22, 2022.

Hansen, Steffen Bo (Technic and Logistics Coordinator at University of Copenhagen, Niels Bohr Institute), Zoom interview with author, March 23, 2022.

Popp, Trever (Field Manager at the Centre for Ice and Climate, Niels Bohr Institute, University of Copenhagen), Zoom interview with author, March 23, 2022.

Thompson, Ellen, March 23, 2022.

Porter, Stacy, Zoom interview with author, May 20, 2022.

Beaudon, Emilie G. (Senior Research Associate at the Byrd Polar and Climate Research Center), Zoom interview with author, May 20, 2022.

Sierra-Hernández, Roxana (Postdoctoral Scholar at the Byrd Polar and Climate Research Center), Zoom interview with author, May 20, 2022.

Laker, Rachel (NSF Postdoctoral Fellow at the University of Cincinnati), phone conversation with author, June 1, 2022.

Porter, Stacy, June 21, 2022.

Porter, Stacy and Lonnie Thompson, June 28, 2022.

108

Thompson, Lonnie, August 1, 2022.

Thompson, Ellen, August 2, 2022.

Thompson, Lonnie, August 2, 2022.

Laker, Rachel, phone conversation with author, October 10, 2022.

Laker, Rachel, in-person conversation with author, October 29, 2022.

Van Vleet, Matthew (BS in Physics, Miami University), in-person conversation with author, October 29, 2022.

Nunn, Richard (Assistant Curator at the National Science Foundation Ice Core Facility), November 21, 2022.

Porter, Stacy, November, 22, 2022.

Nunn, Richard, November 28, 2022.

Nunn, Richard, November 29, 2022.

Van Vleet, Matthew, phone conversation with author, November 30, 2022.

Nunn, Richard, December 8, 2022.

Nunn, Richard, December 15, 2022.

Laker, Rachel, phone conversation with author, February 8, 2023.

Nunn, Richard, February 22, 2023.

Laker, Rachel and Matthew Van Vleet, phone conversation with author, February 22, 2023.

PHOTO CREDITS

Dr. Bernhard Bereiter / Empa: Cover

Liz Crawford: Back cover

Diamond20, courtesy of Wikimedia Commons: 12

Elaine Hood / USAP Photo Library: i, 6–7, 11, 52, 79

Mike Lucibella / USAP Photo Library: 27, 43, 47, 73

Ellen Mosley-Thompson: 57 bottom, 74

NASA/Cindy Evans: 71

NASA/Goddard Space Flight Center Scientific Visualization Studio: 28, 29

NASA/World Wind: 35

Peter Neff: 87

Mindy Nicewonger: 23, 94

Erich Osterberg / NOAA: 91

Steven Profaizer / USAP Photo Library: 21, 57 top

Boris Radosavljevic, courtesy of Wikimedia Commons: 17

Peter Rejcek / USAP Photo Library: 2, 61, 81

Joseph Souney: 83, diagram courtesy of NSF-ICF

Emily Stone / USAP Photo Library: 18, 58

Lonnie G. Thompson: 37 top, 37 bottom, 38, 62

Carmella Van Vleet: 15, 63

INDEX

Italic page numbers refer to illustrations.